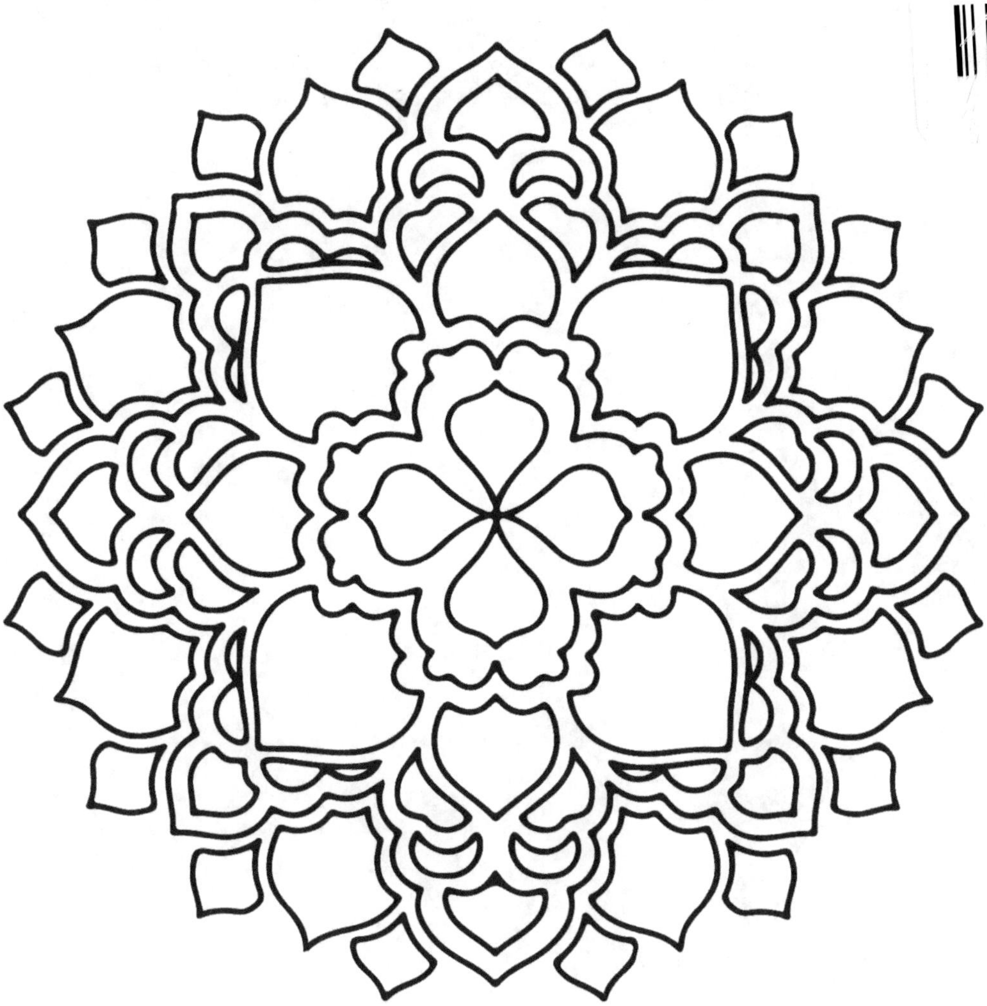

This Coloring Book belongs to:

Color Test Page

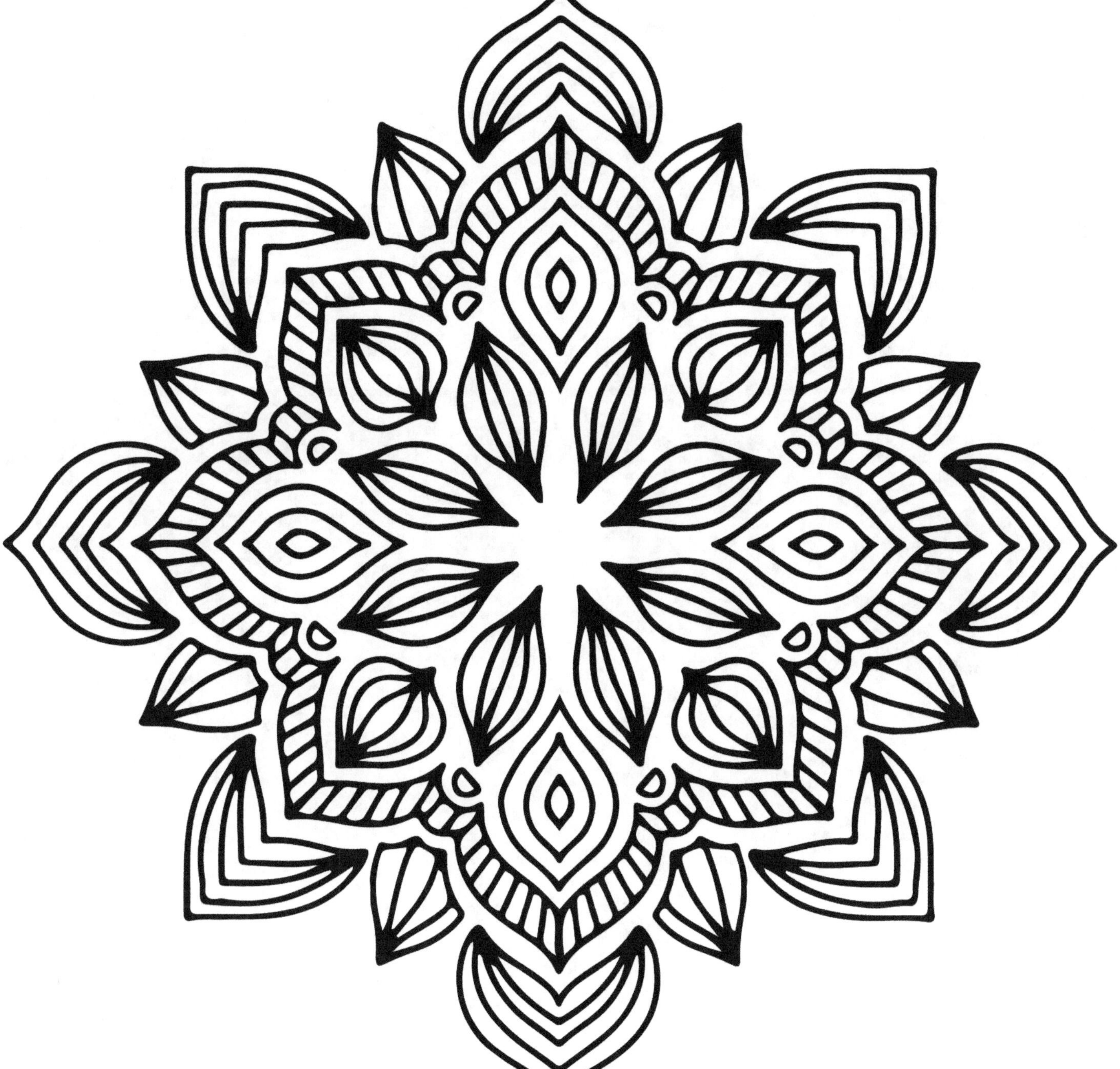

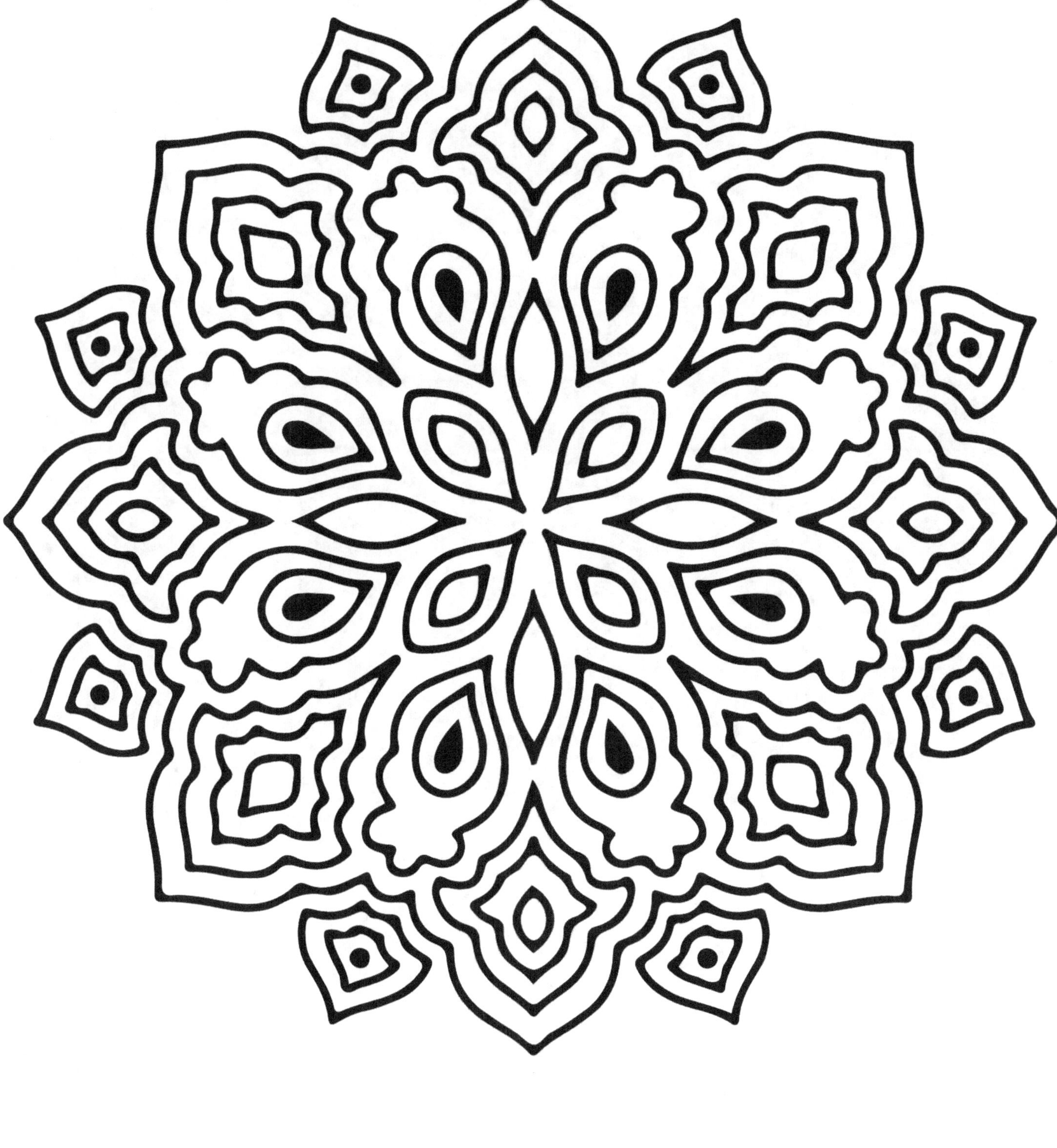

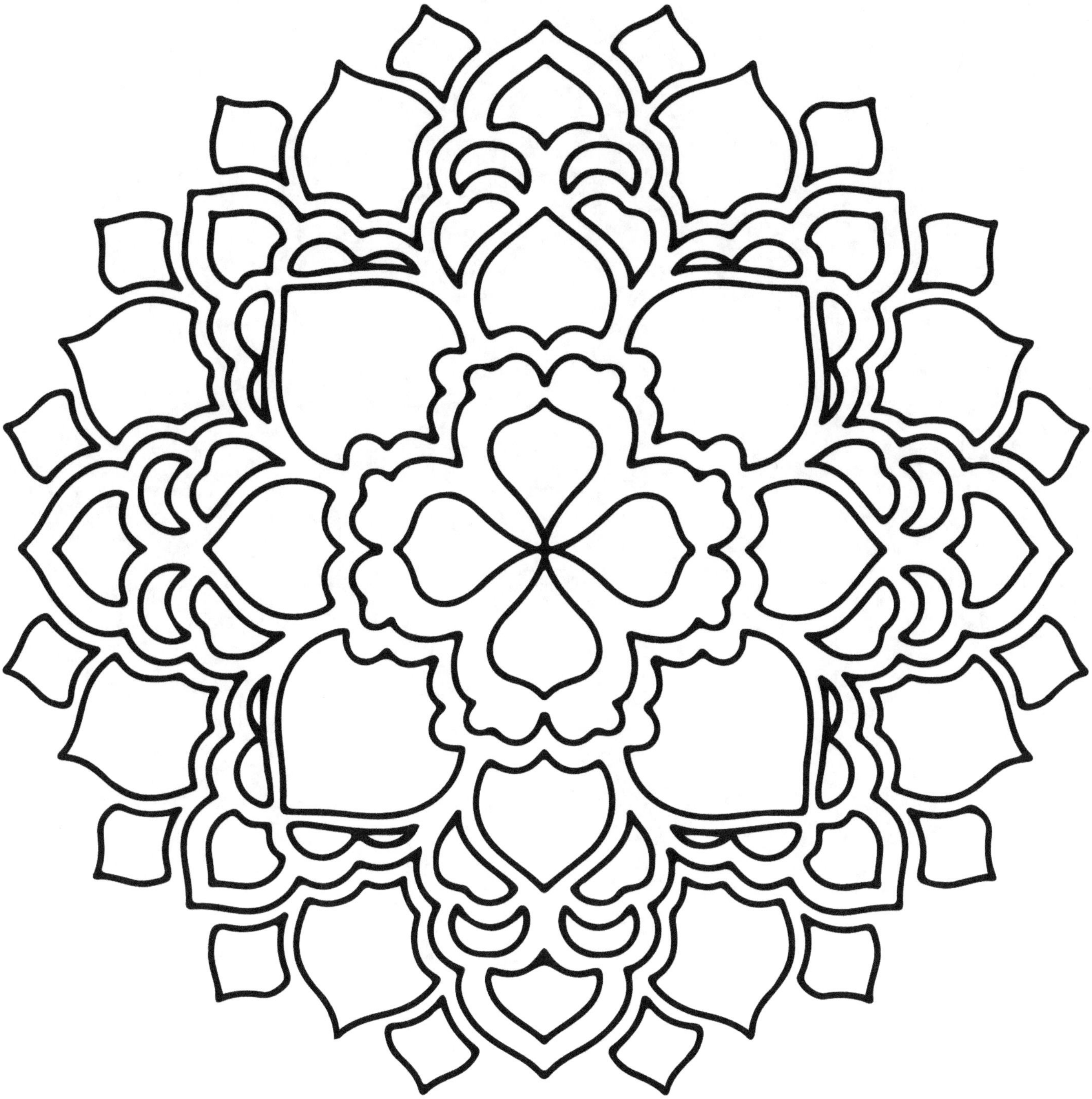

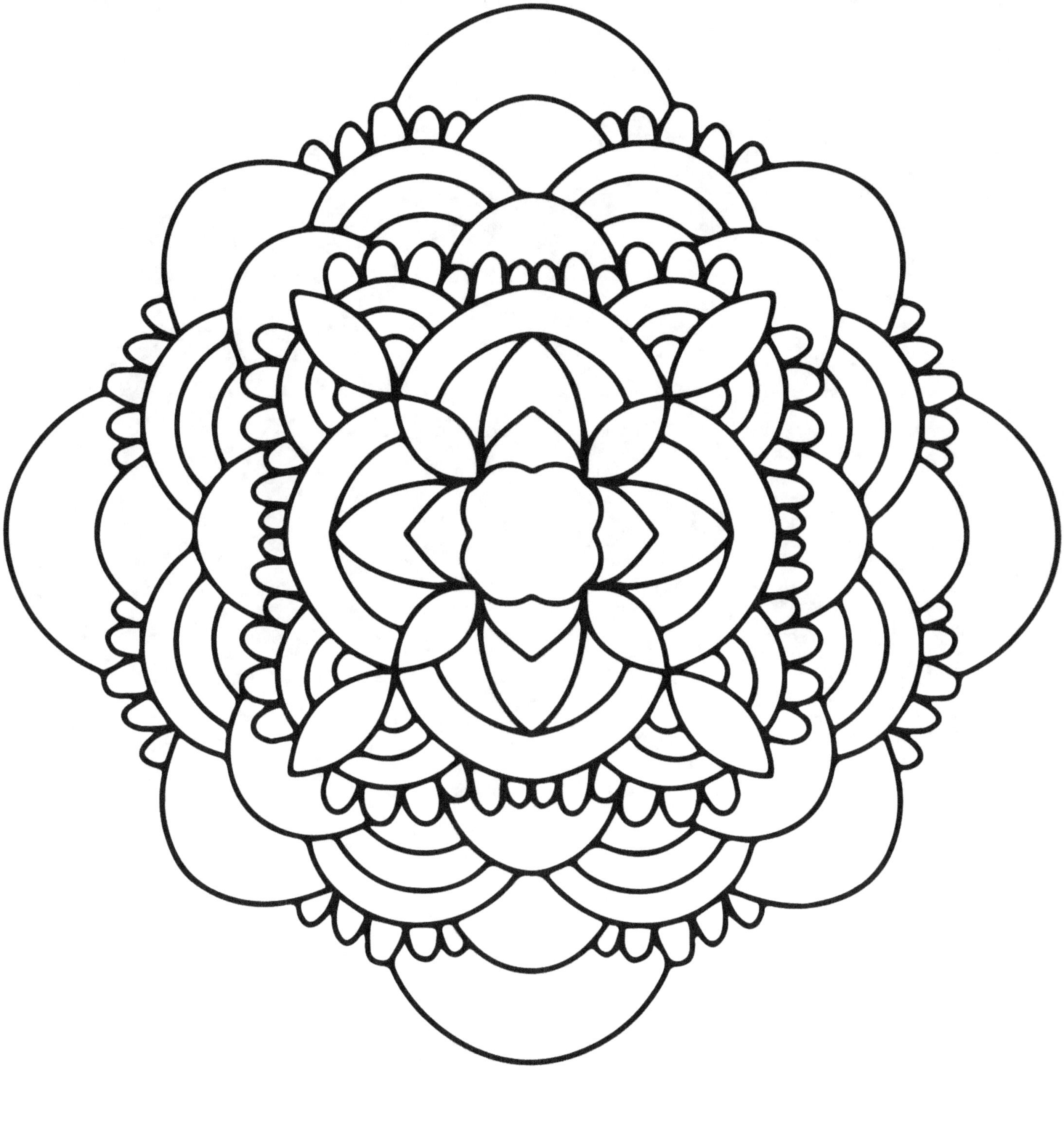

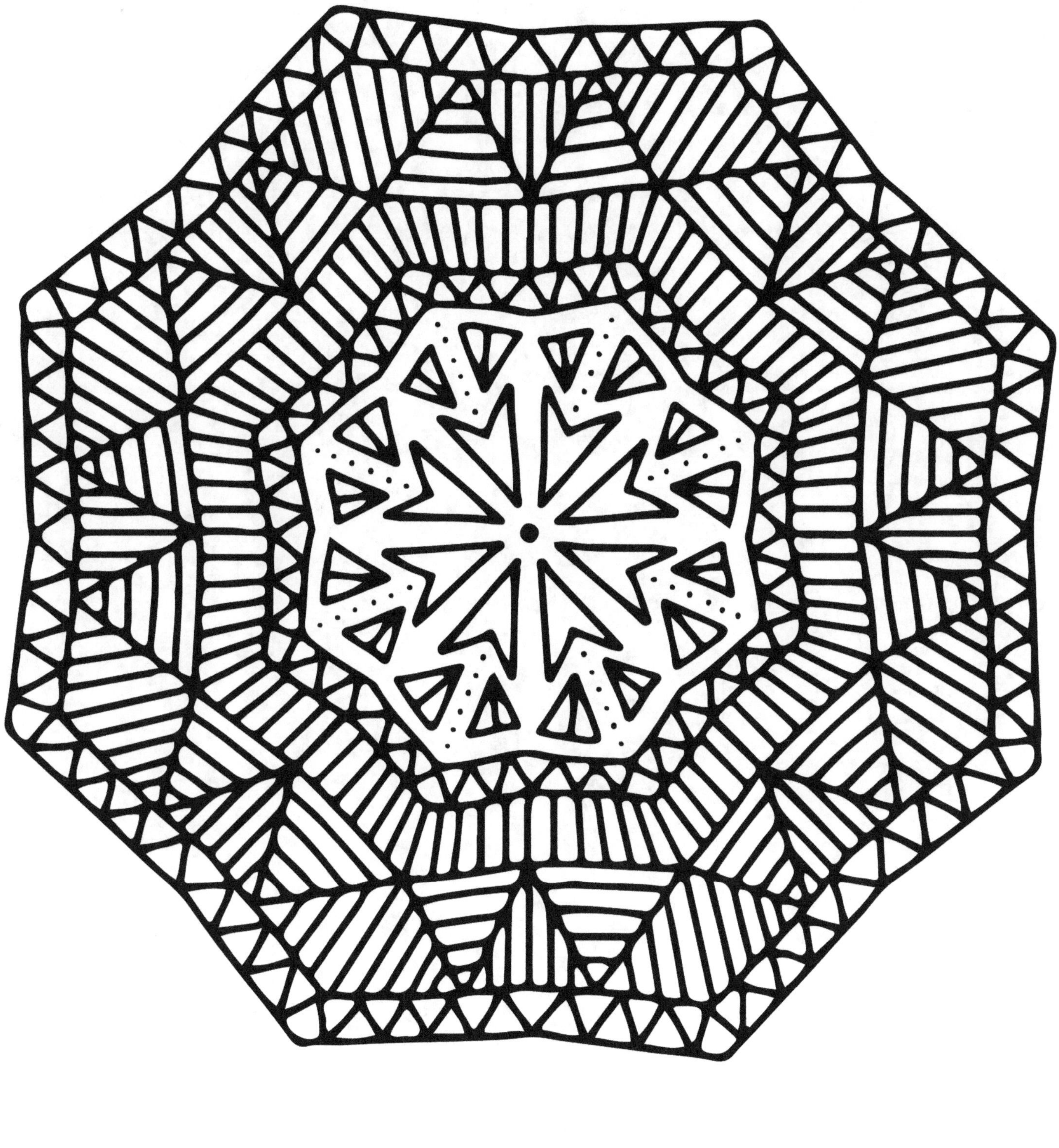

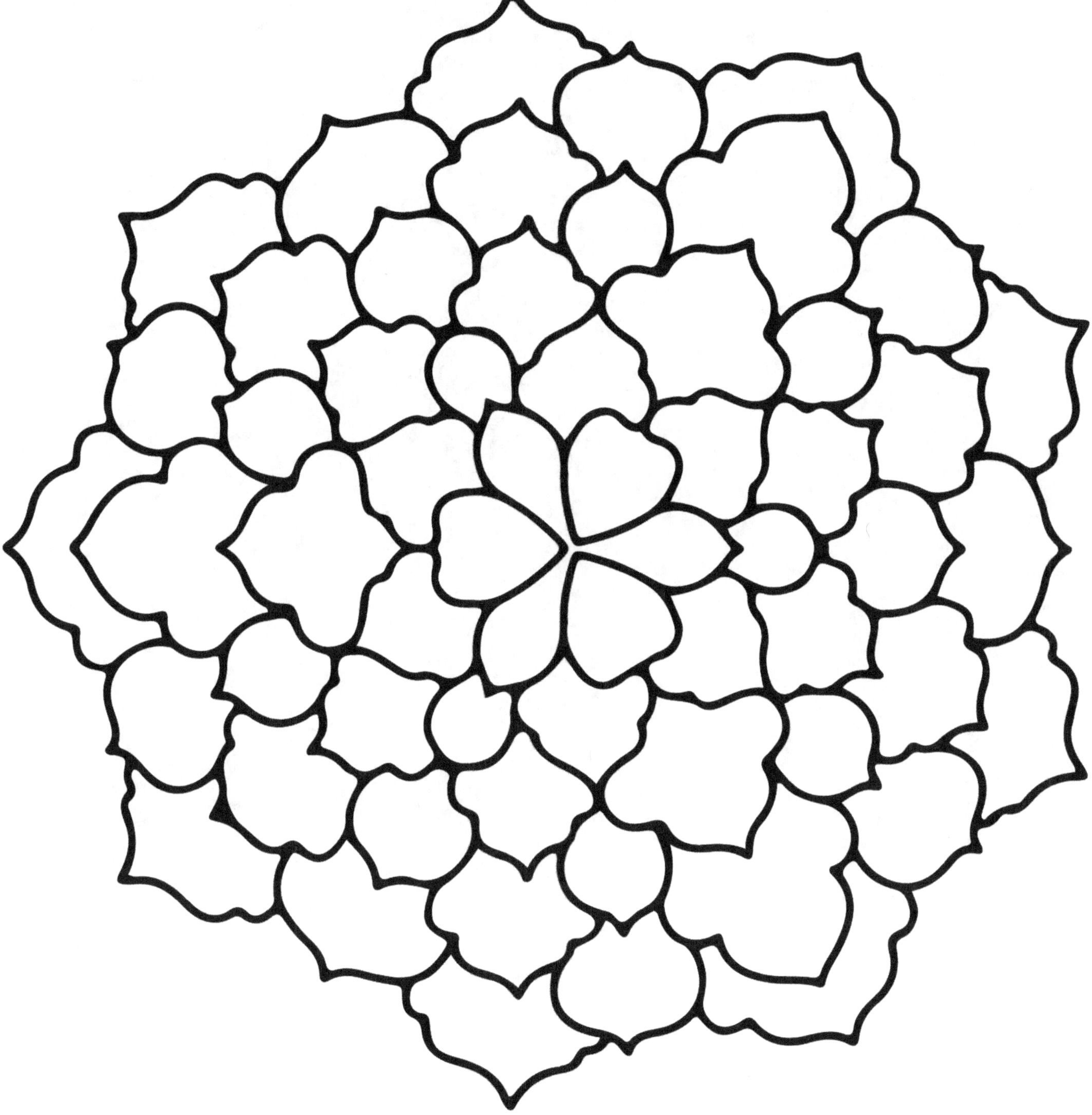

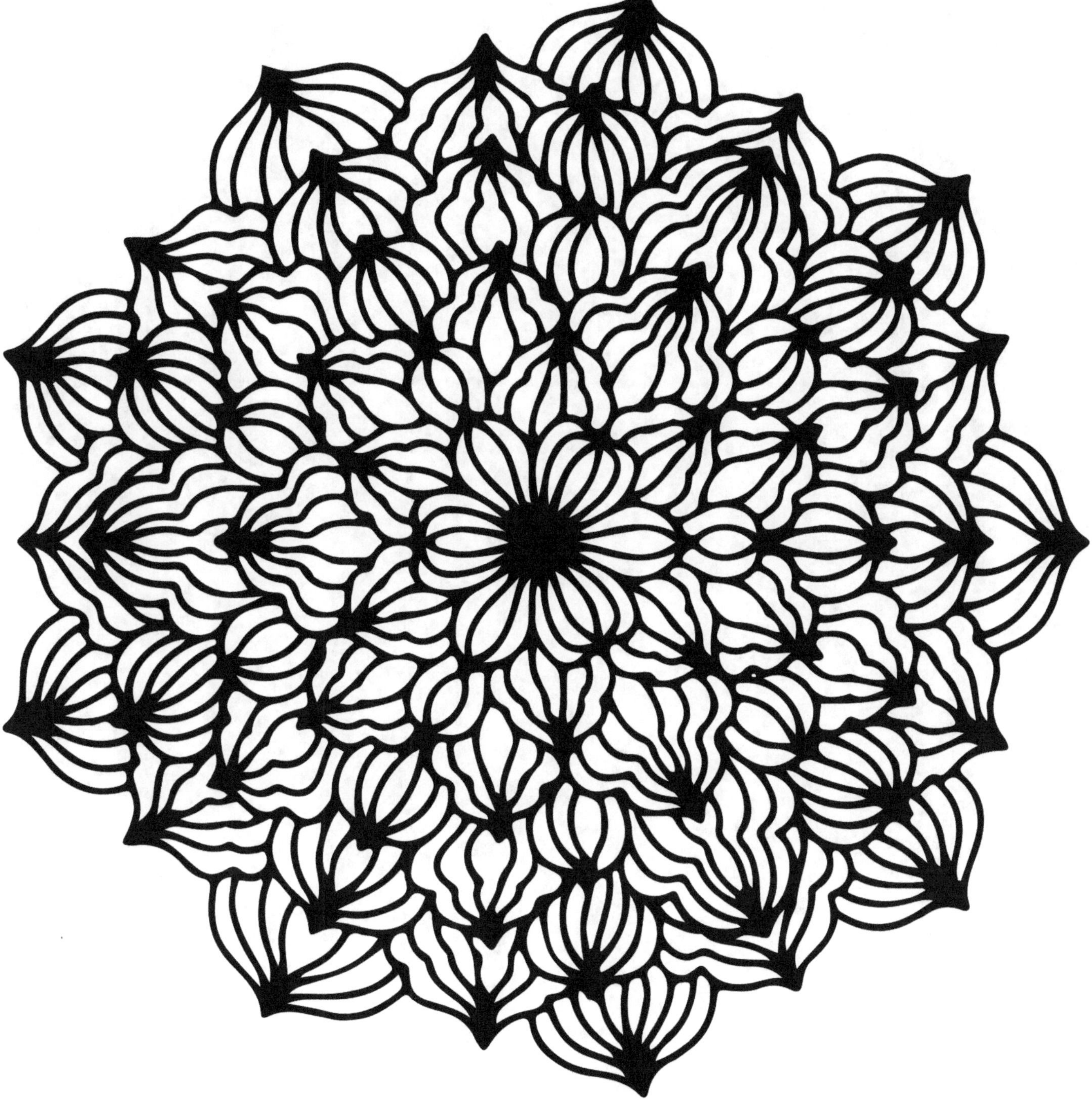

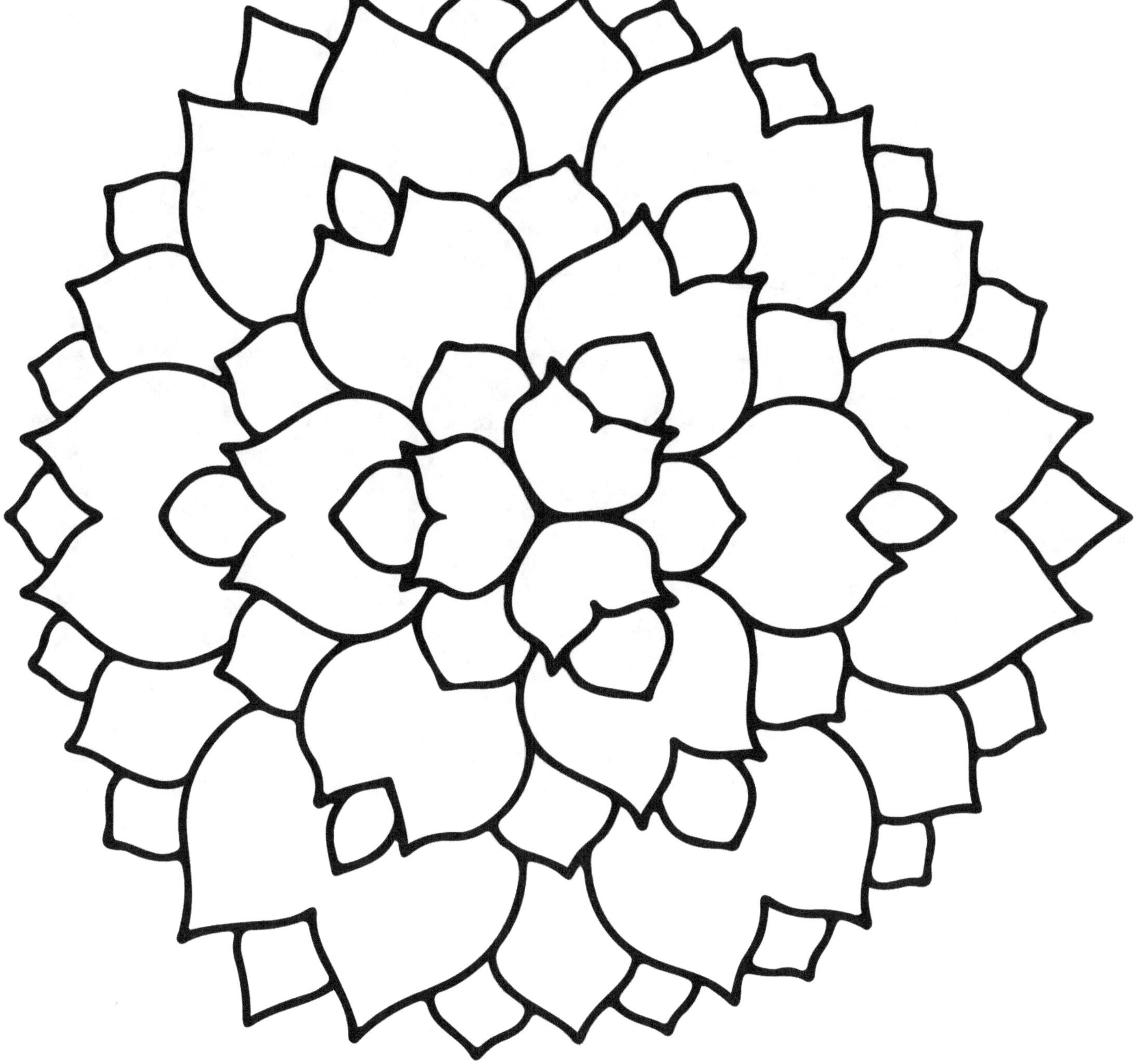

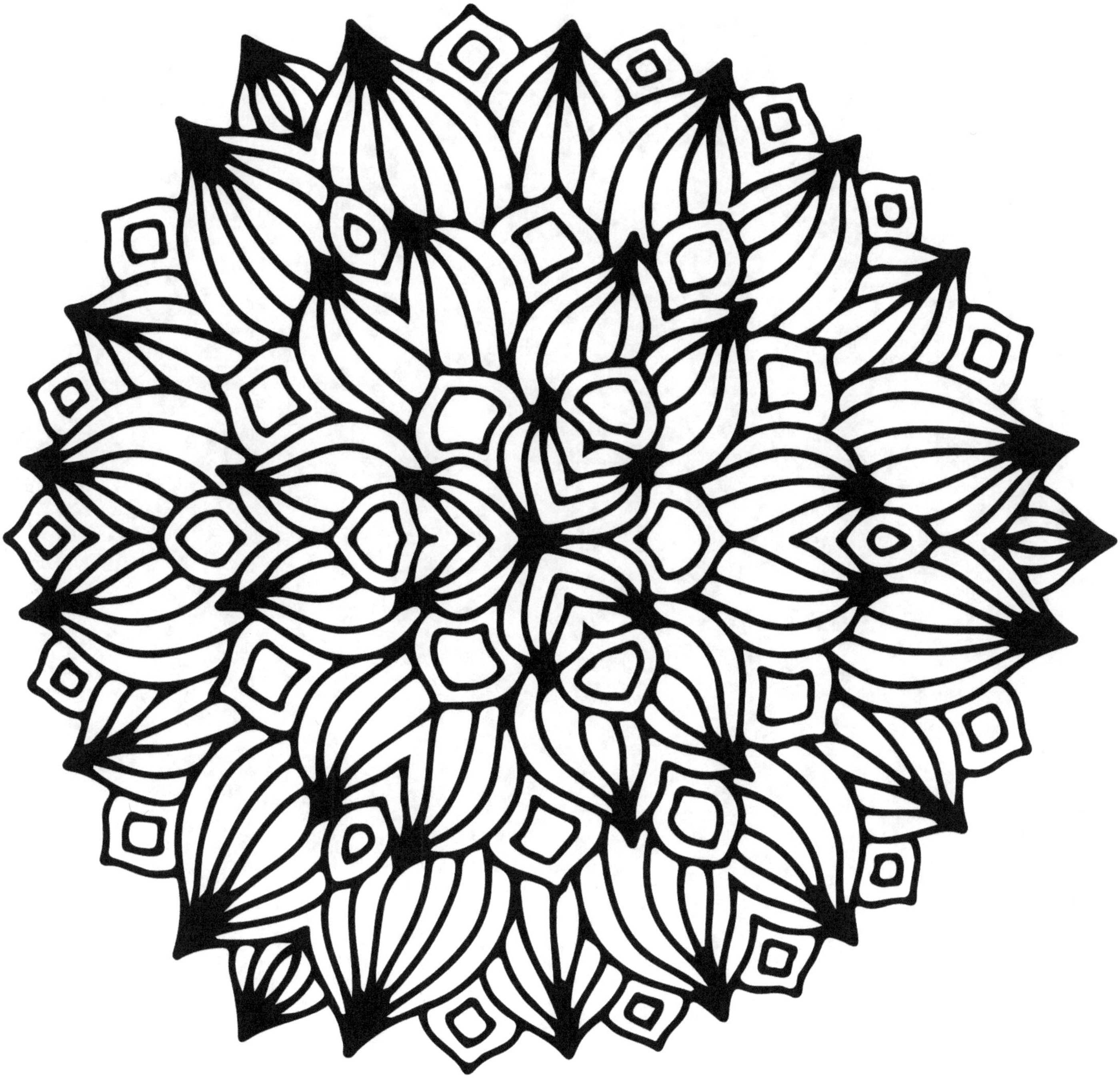

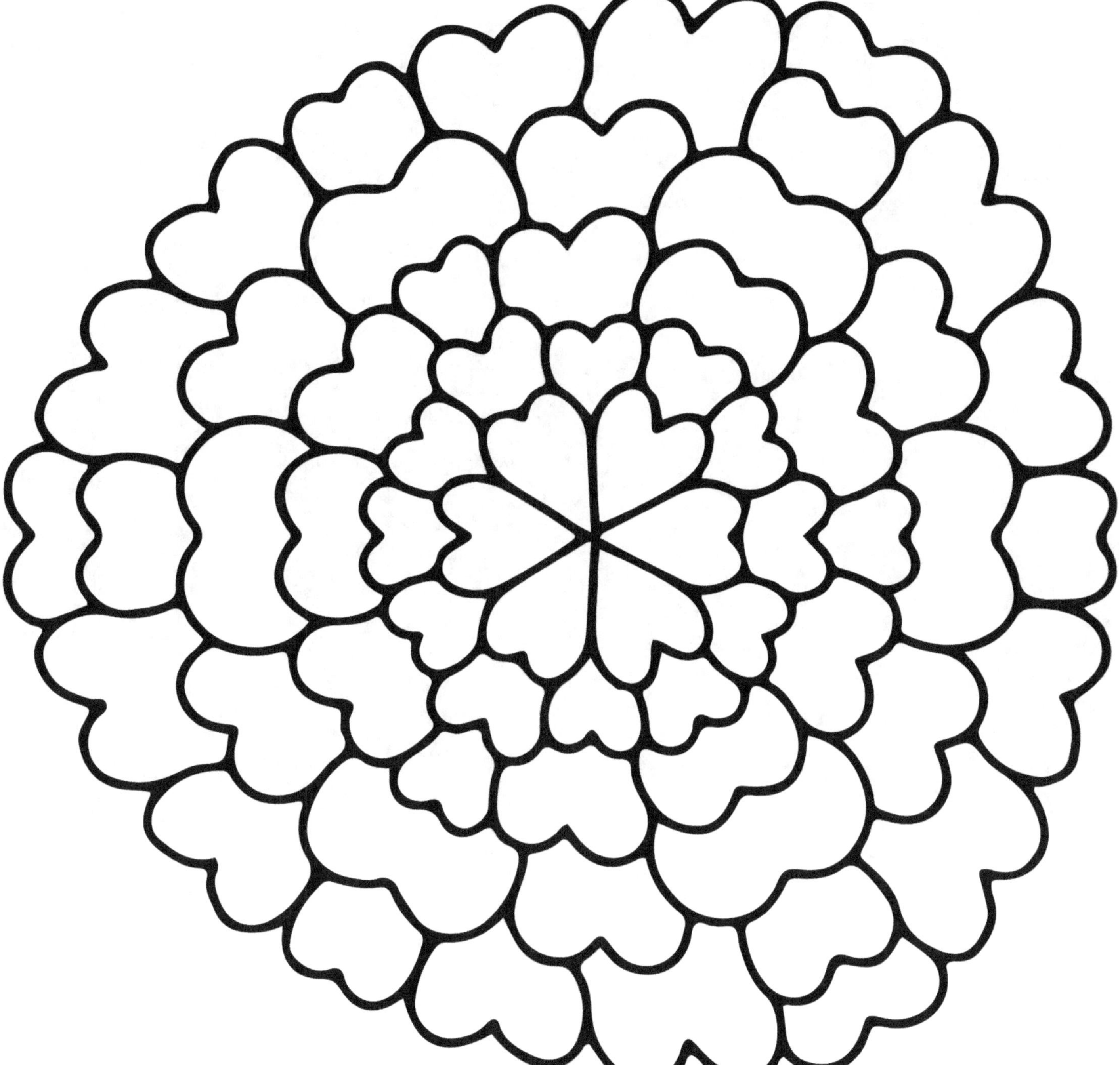

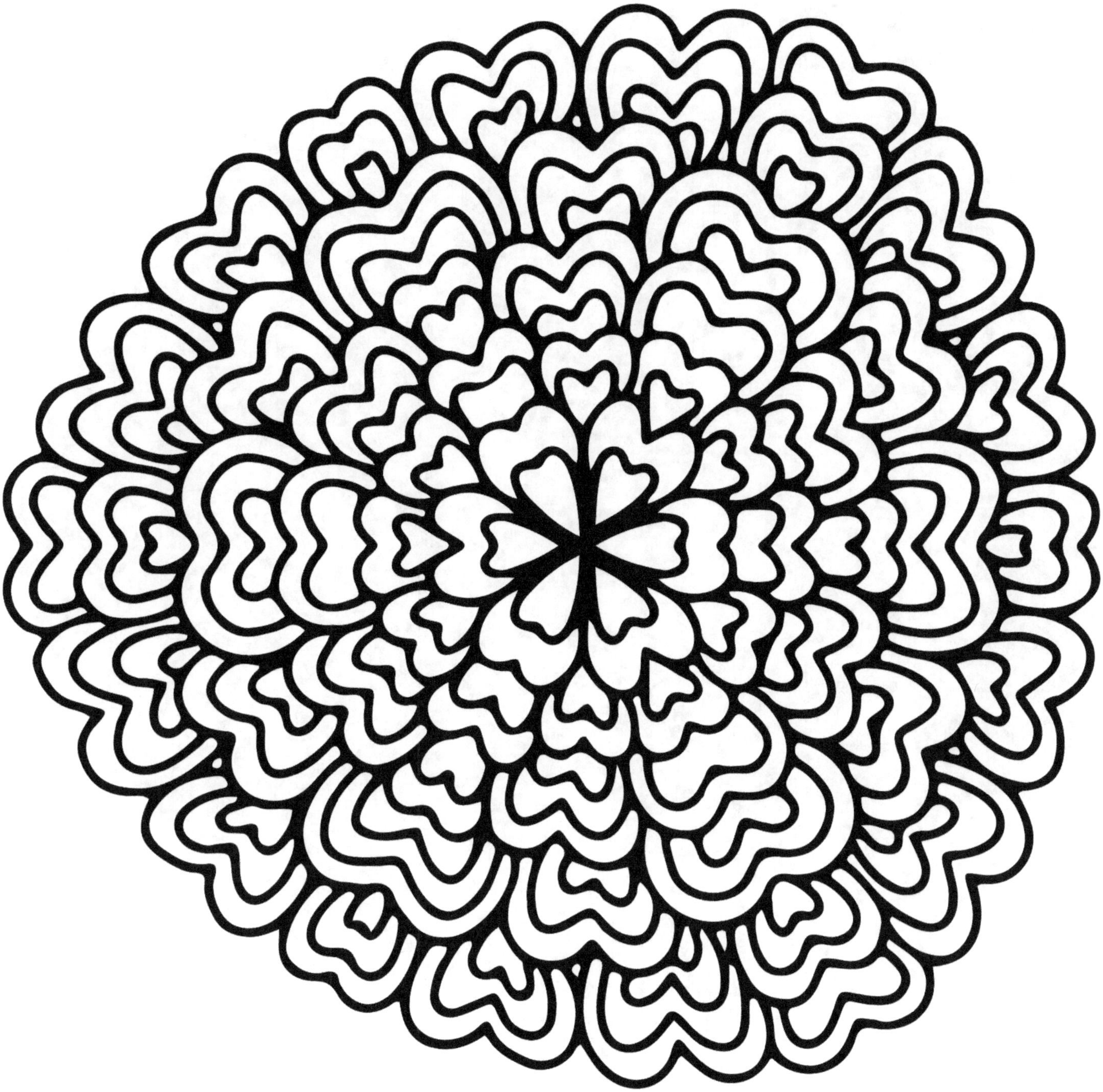

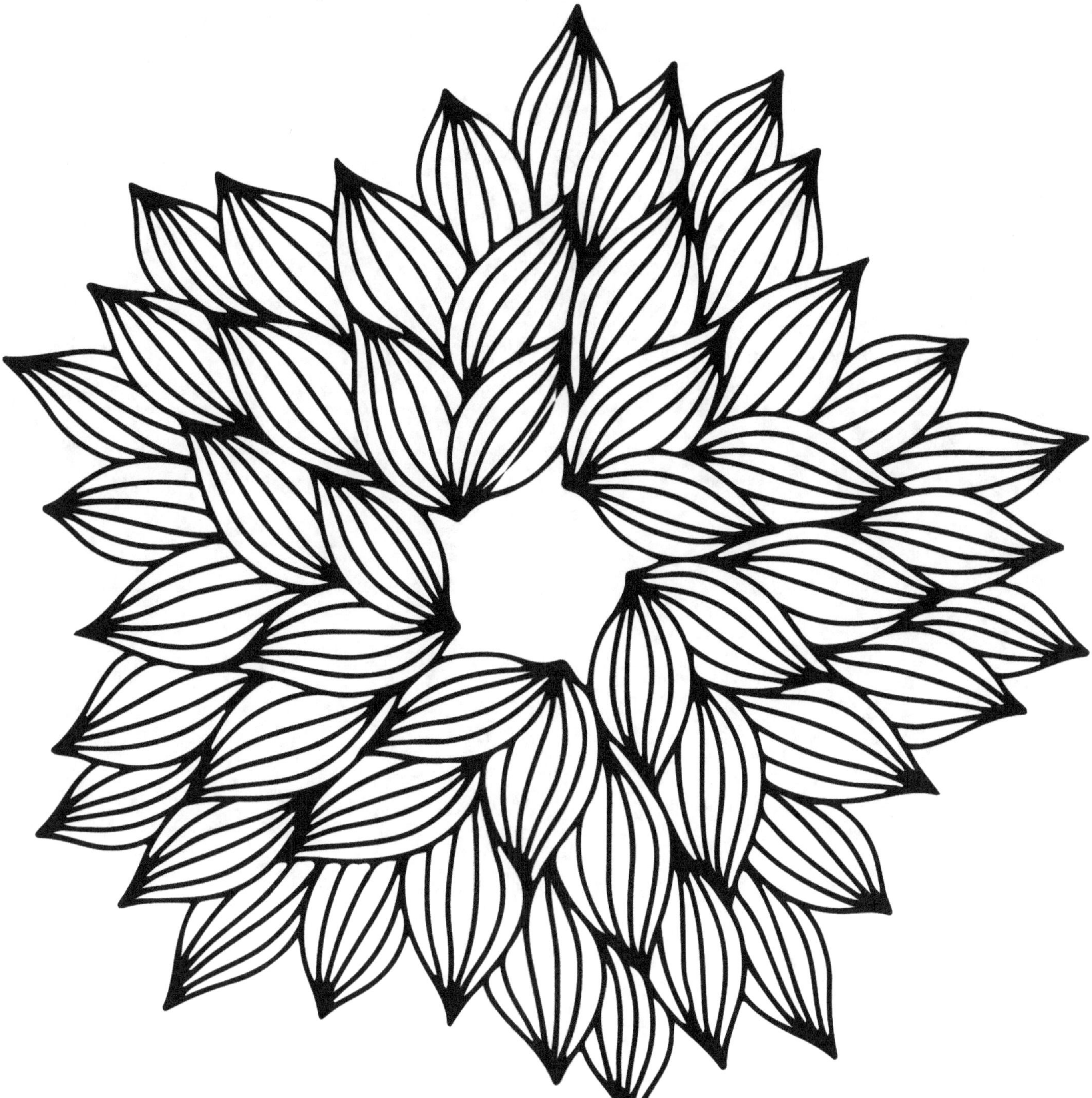

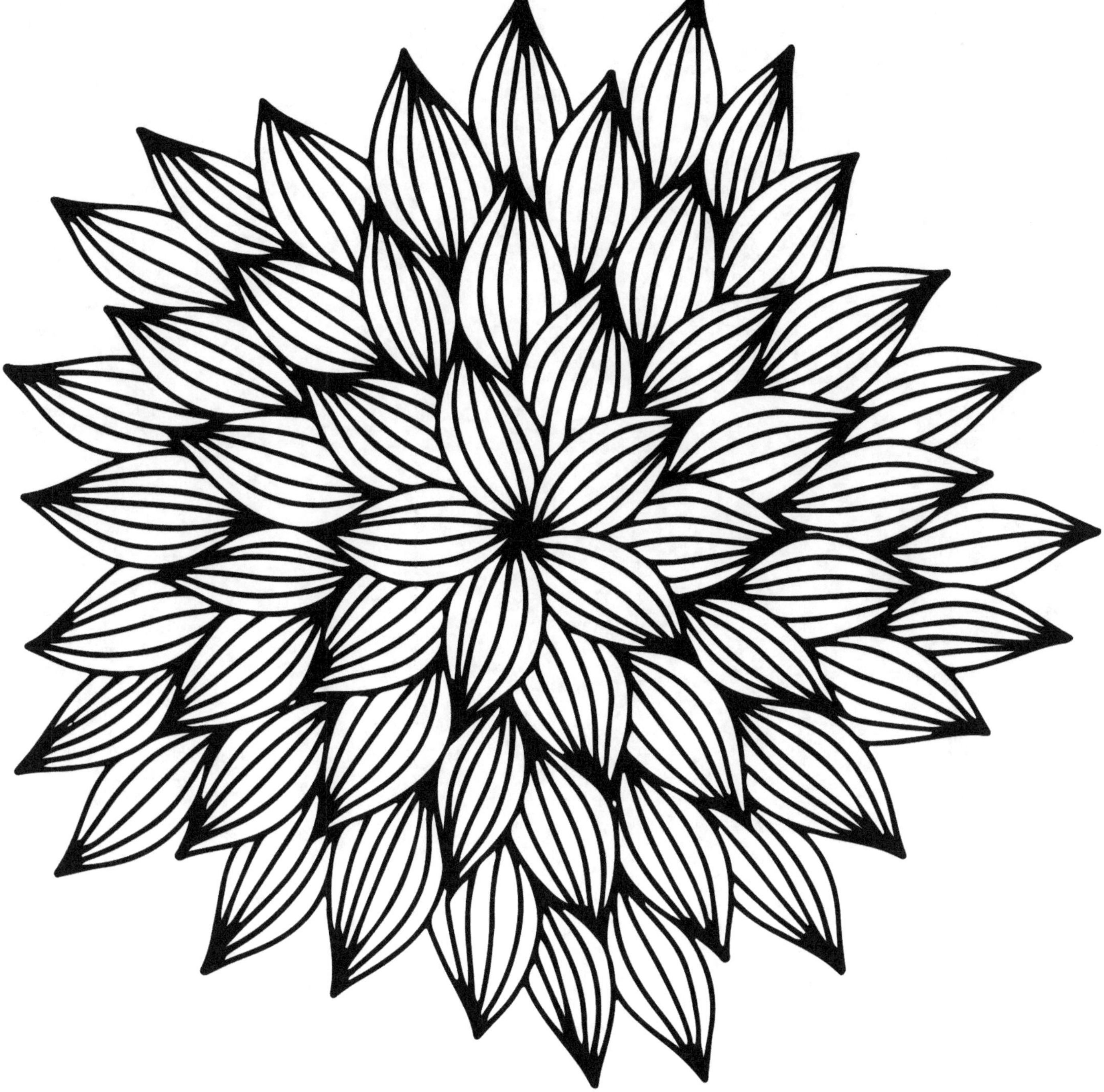

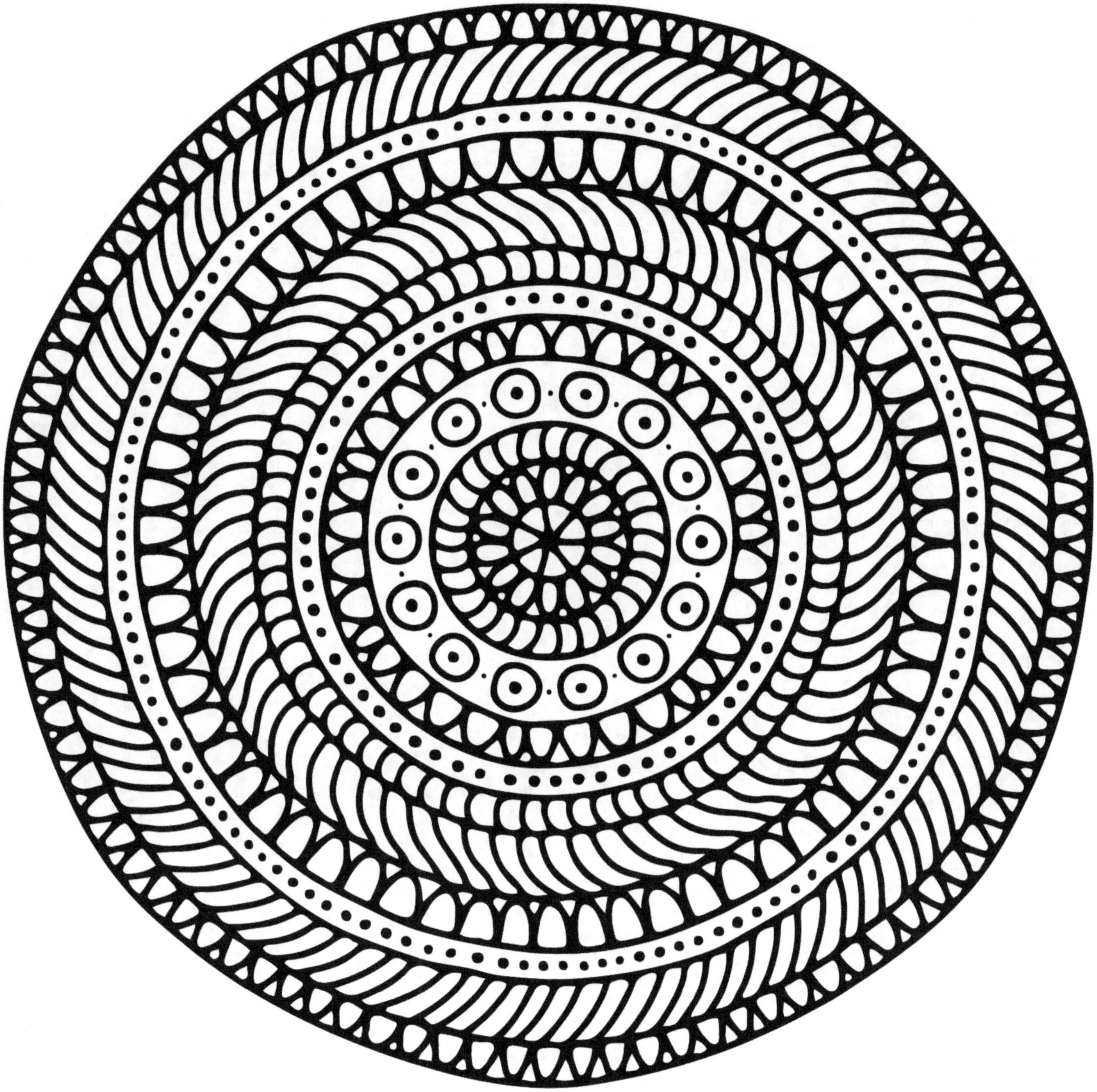

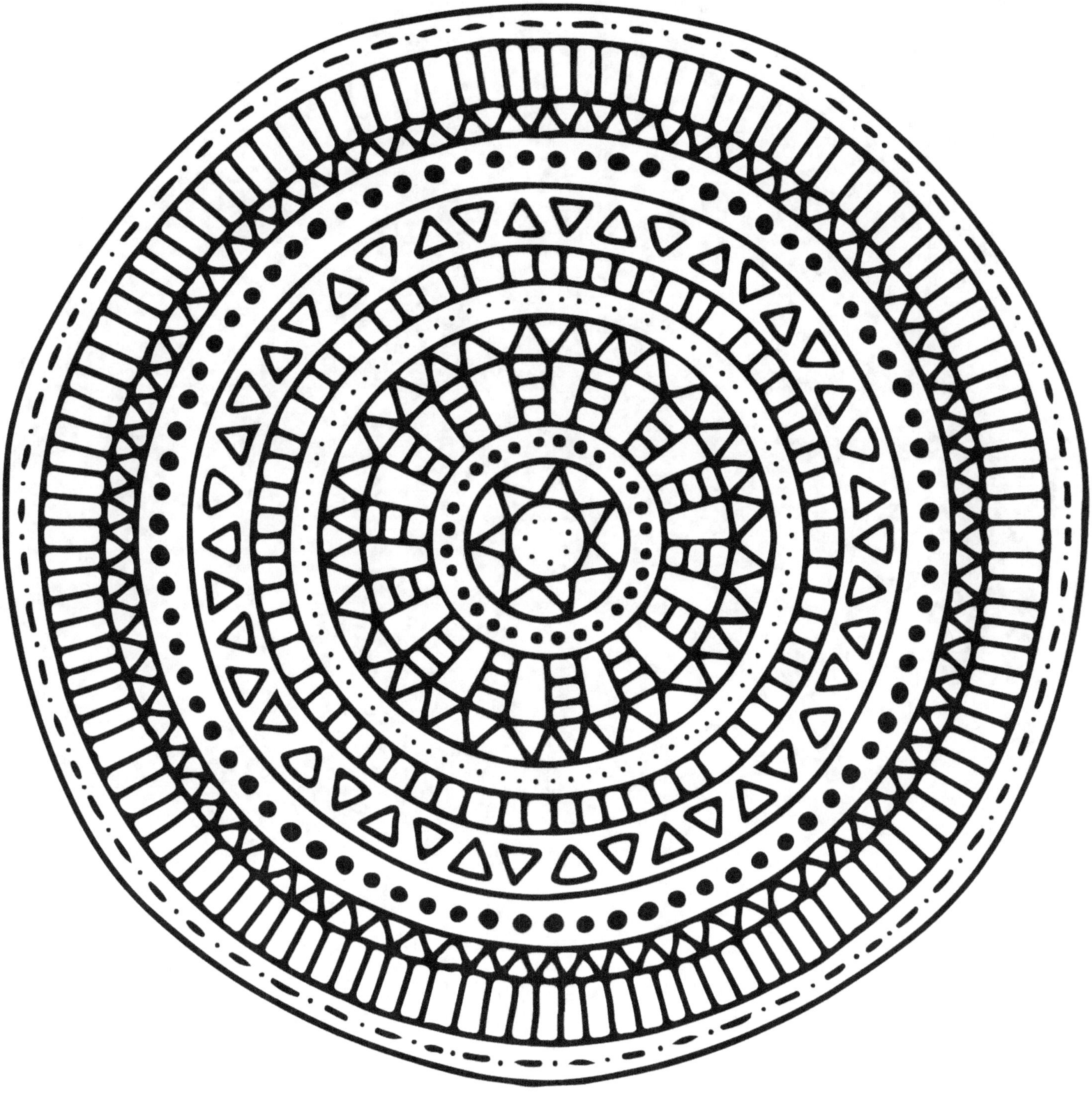

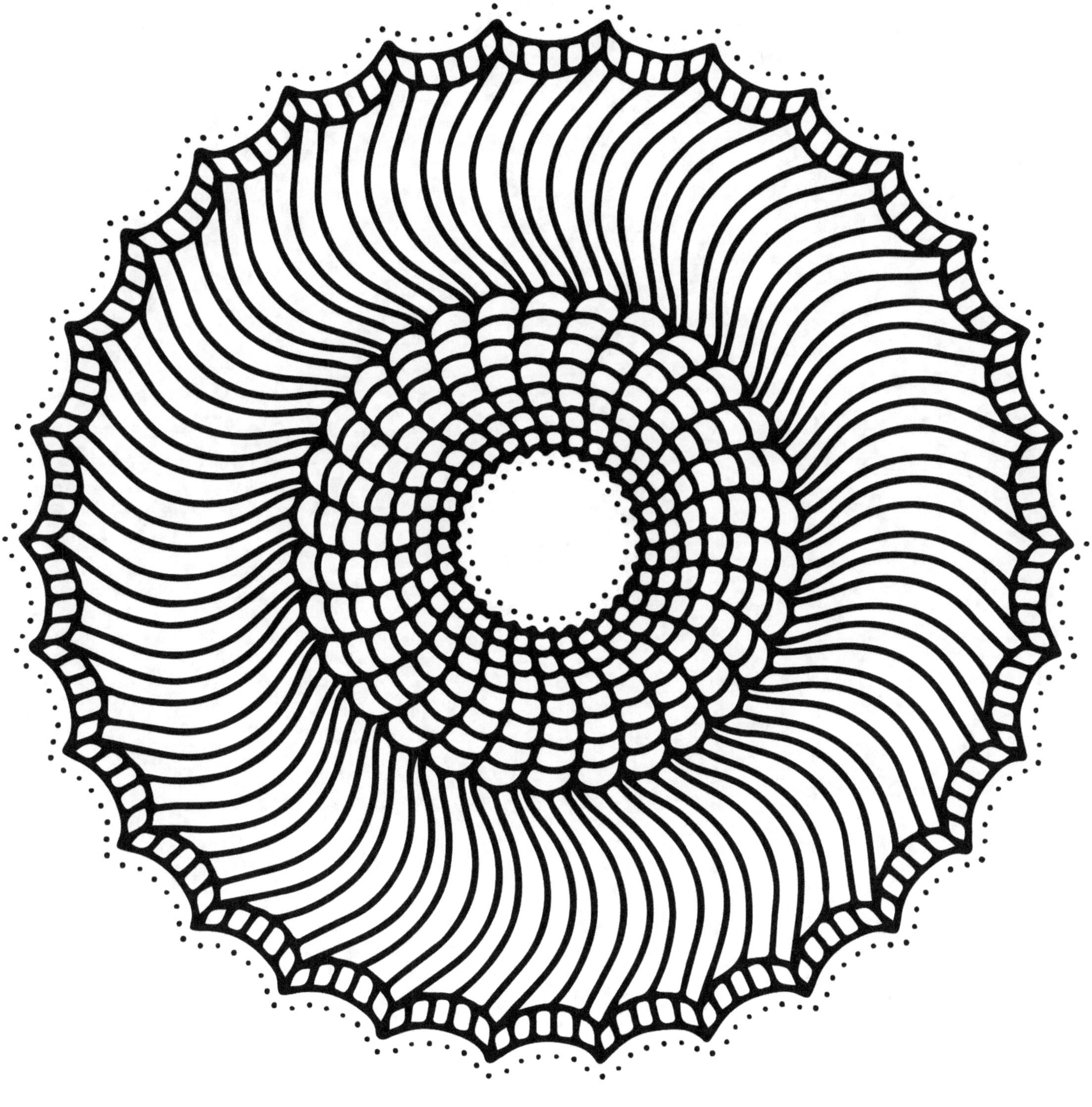

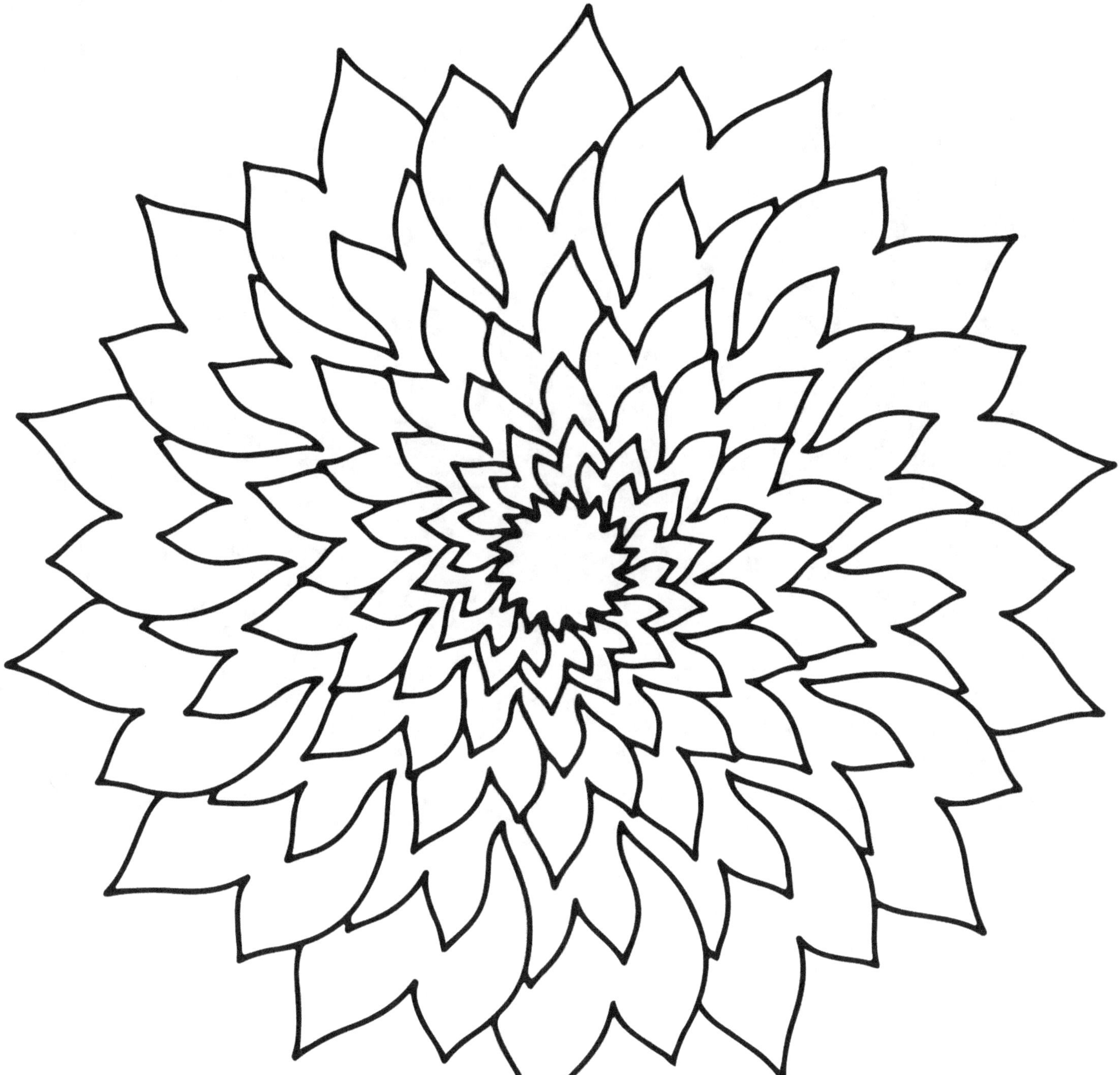

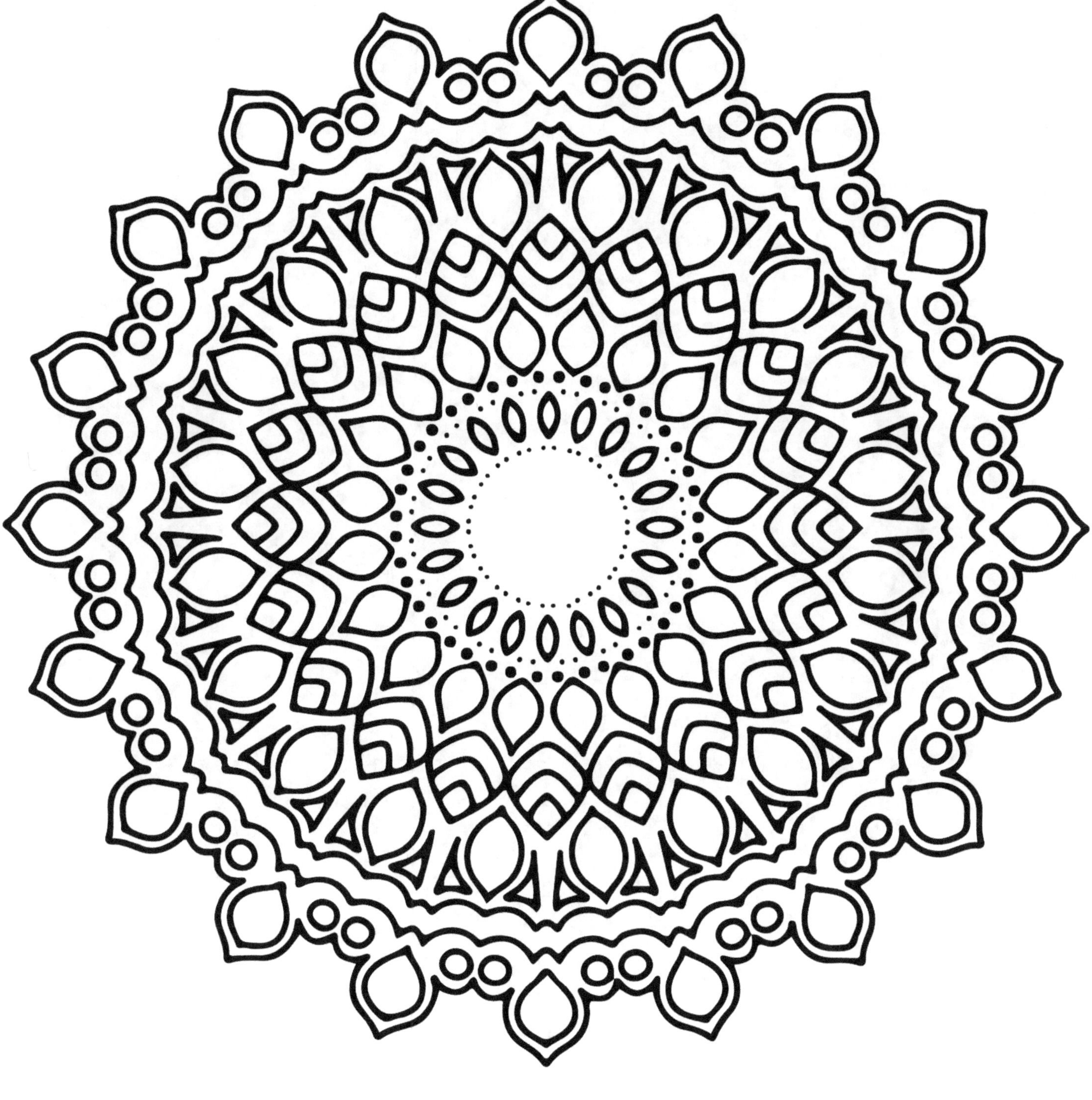

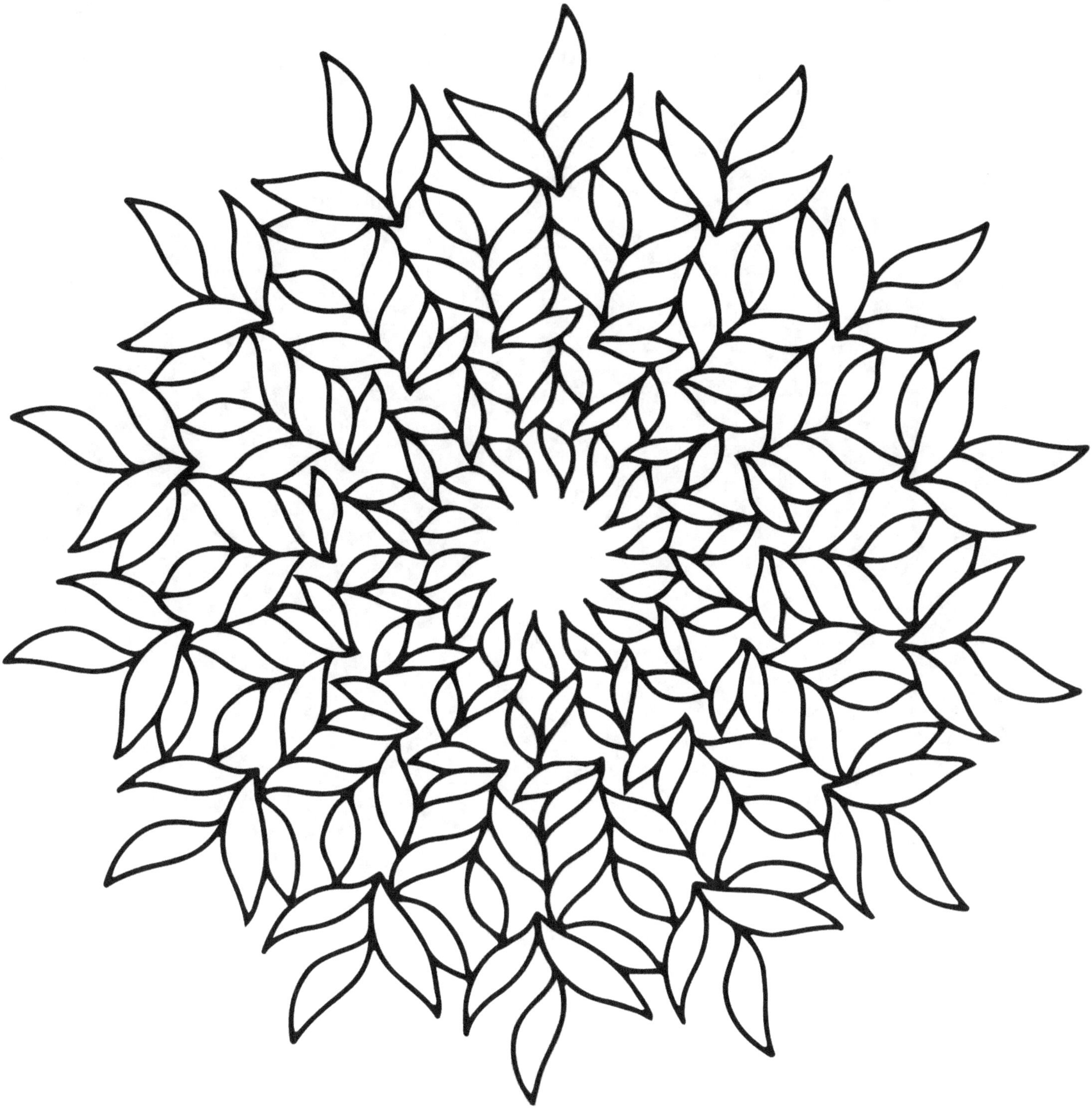

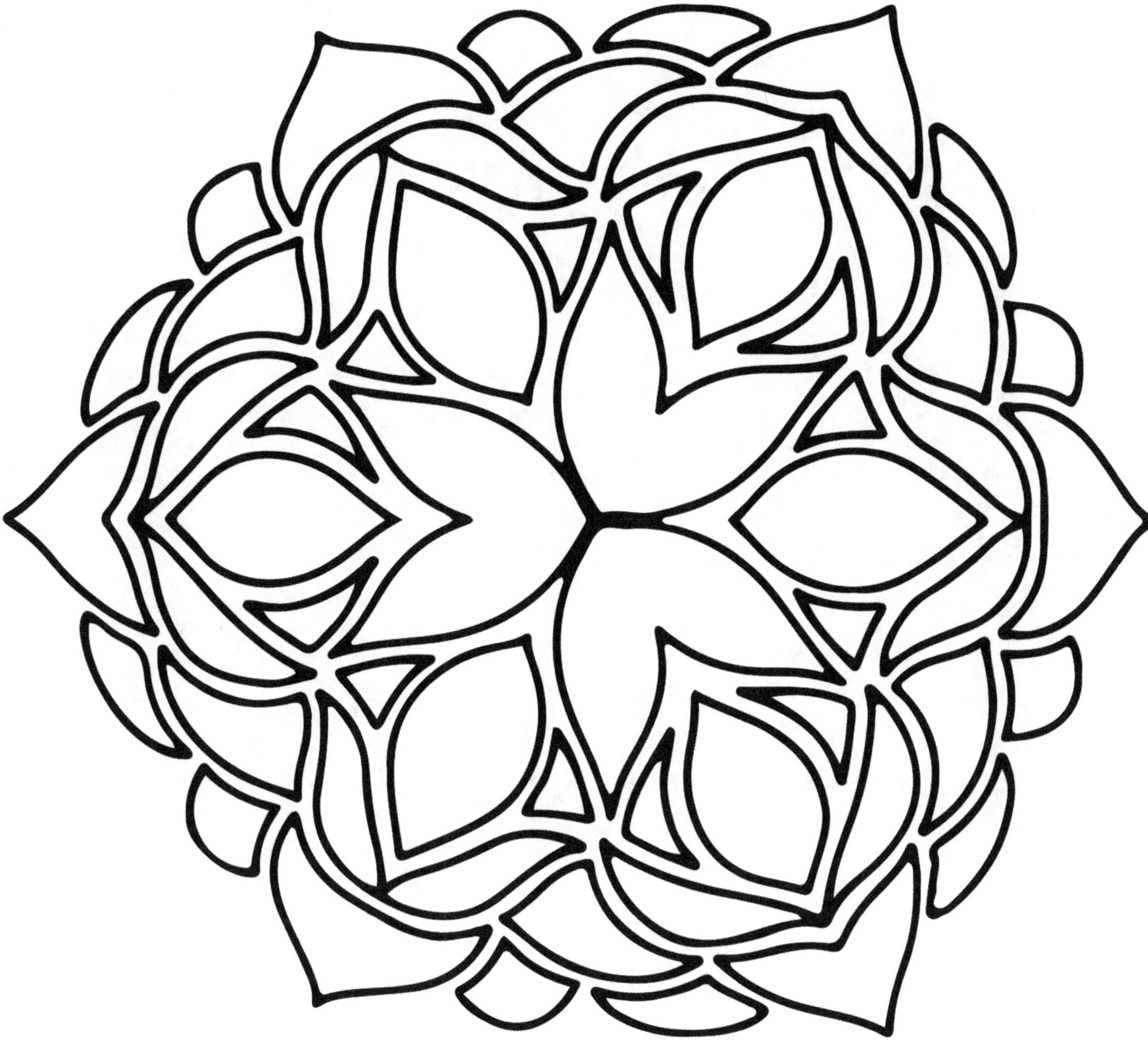

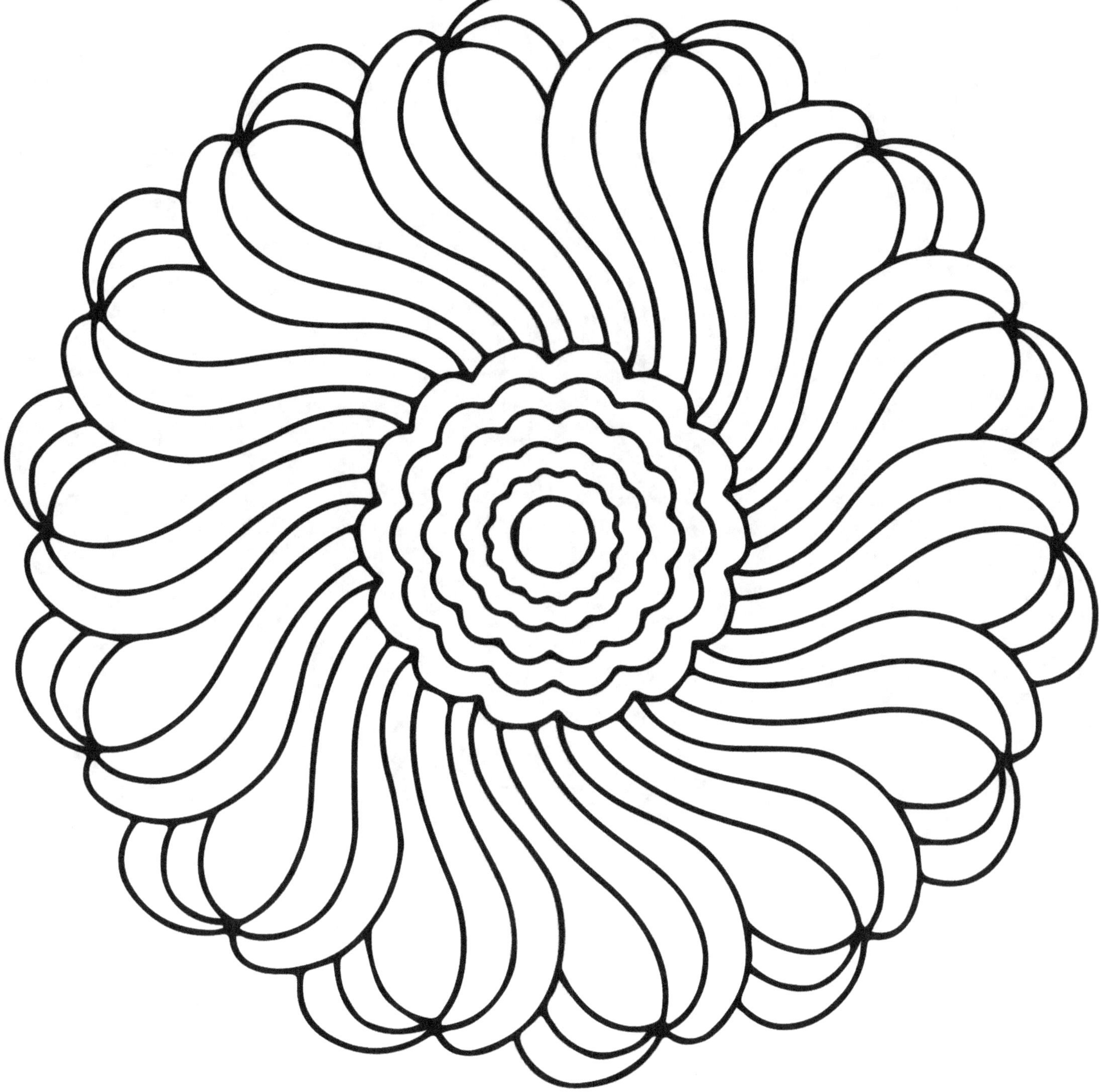

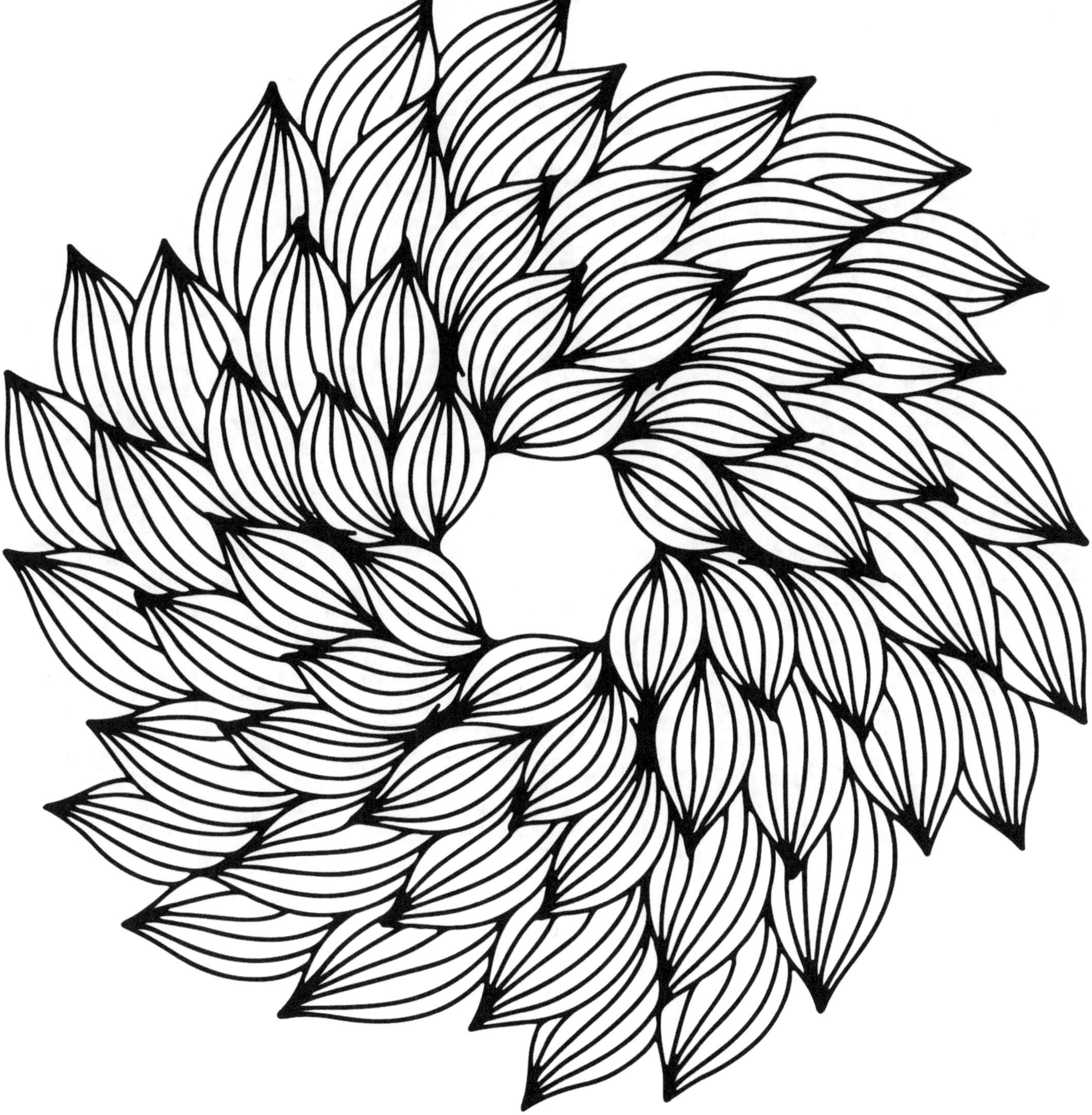

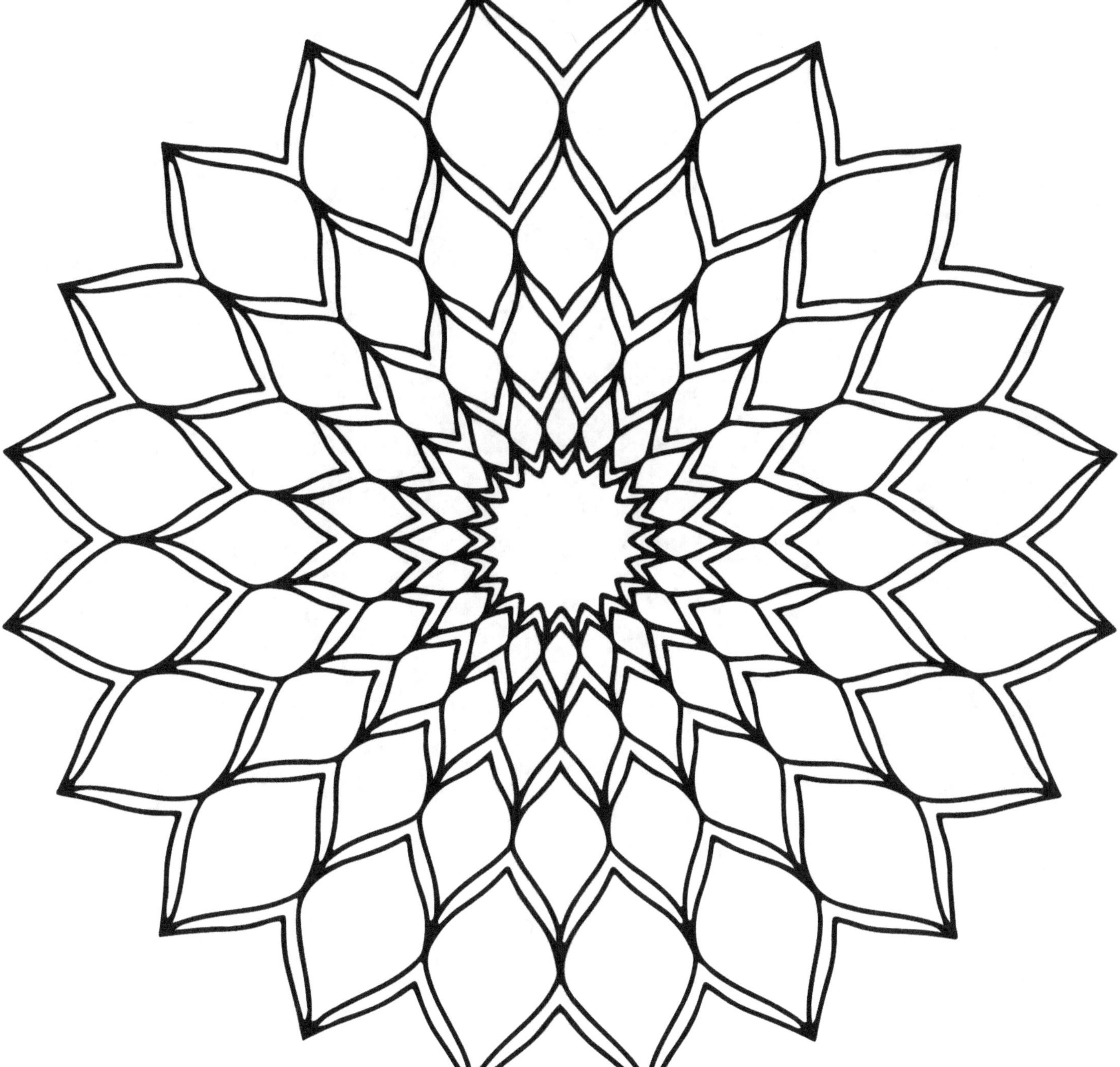

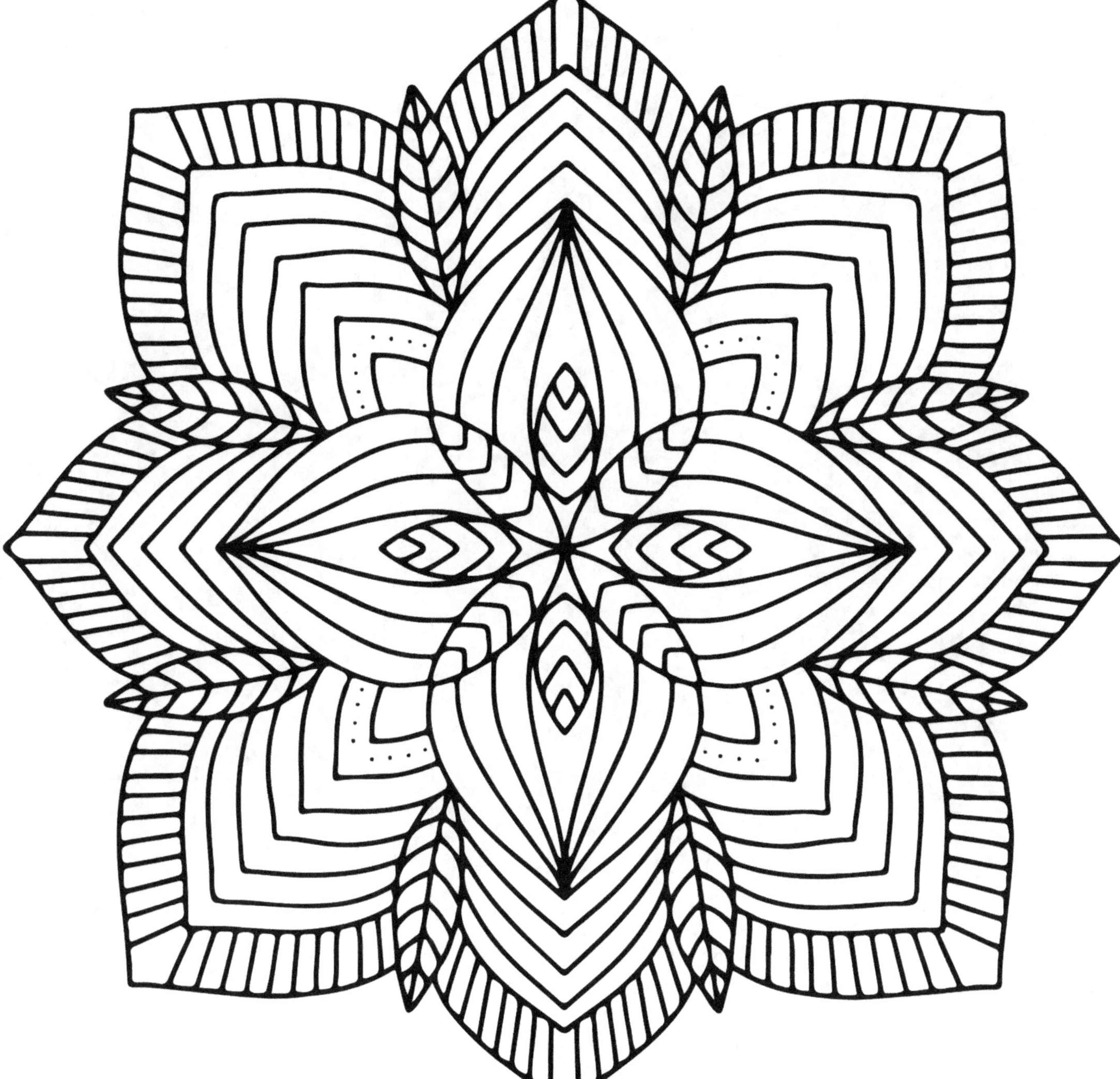

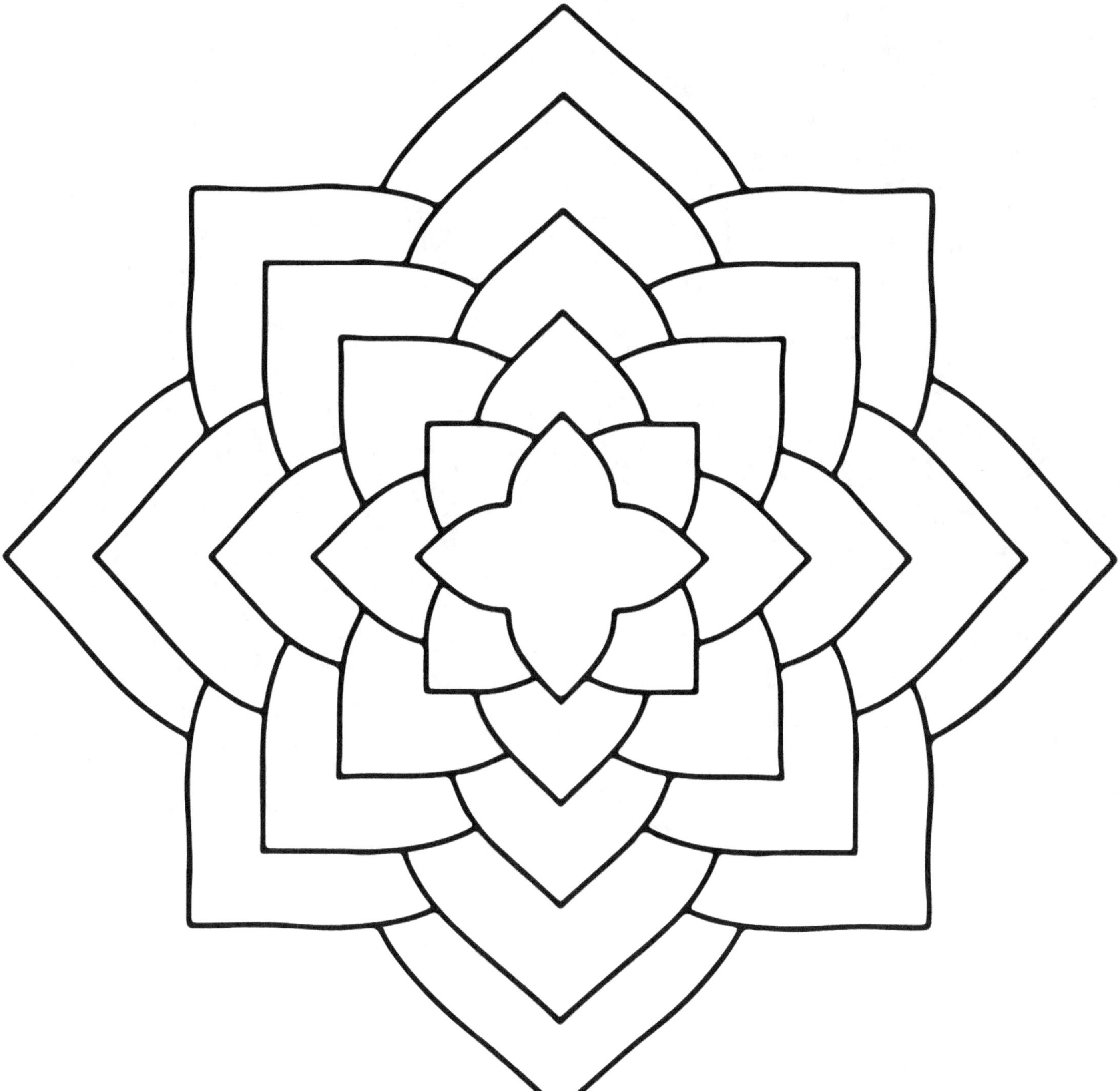

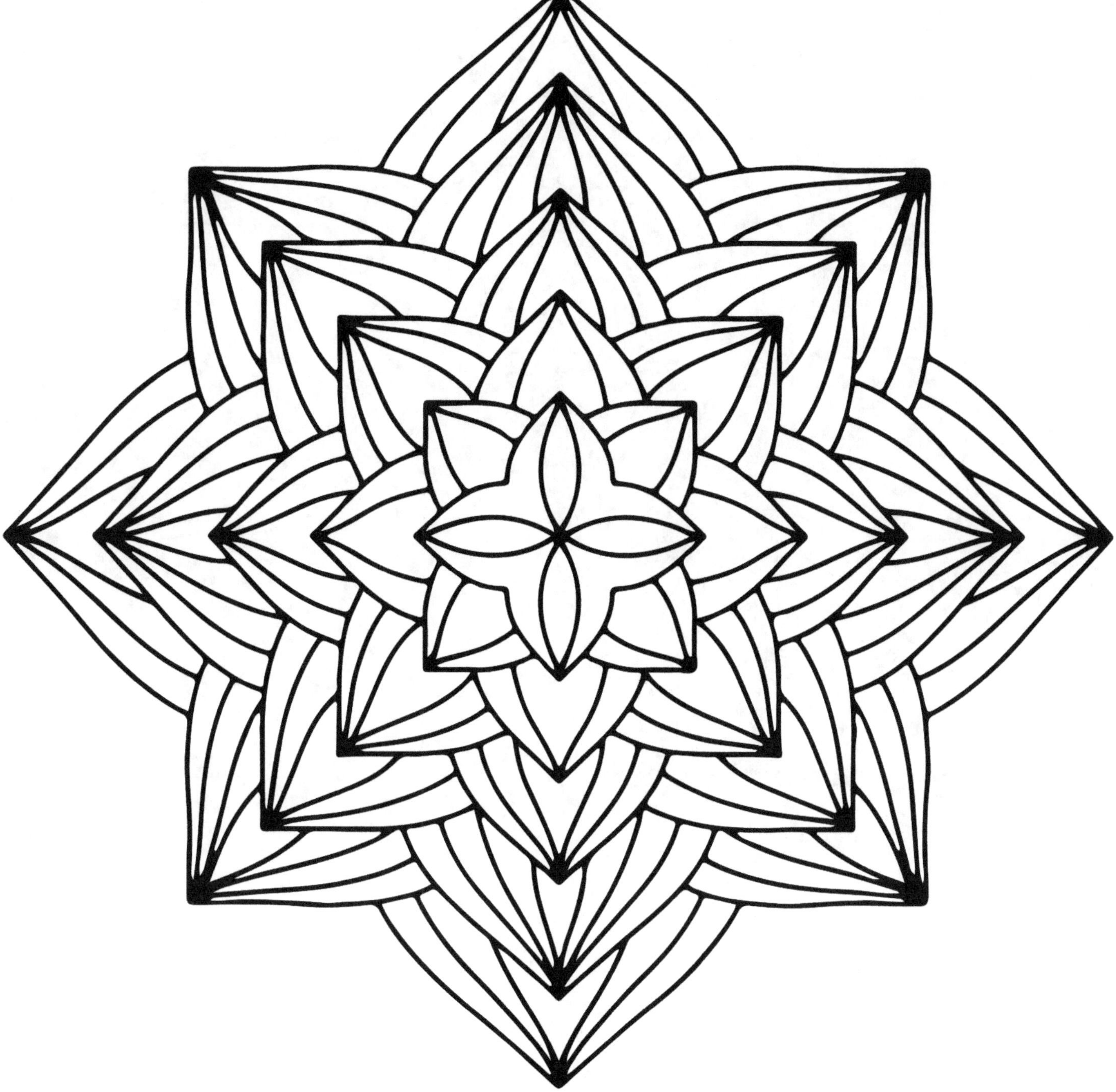

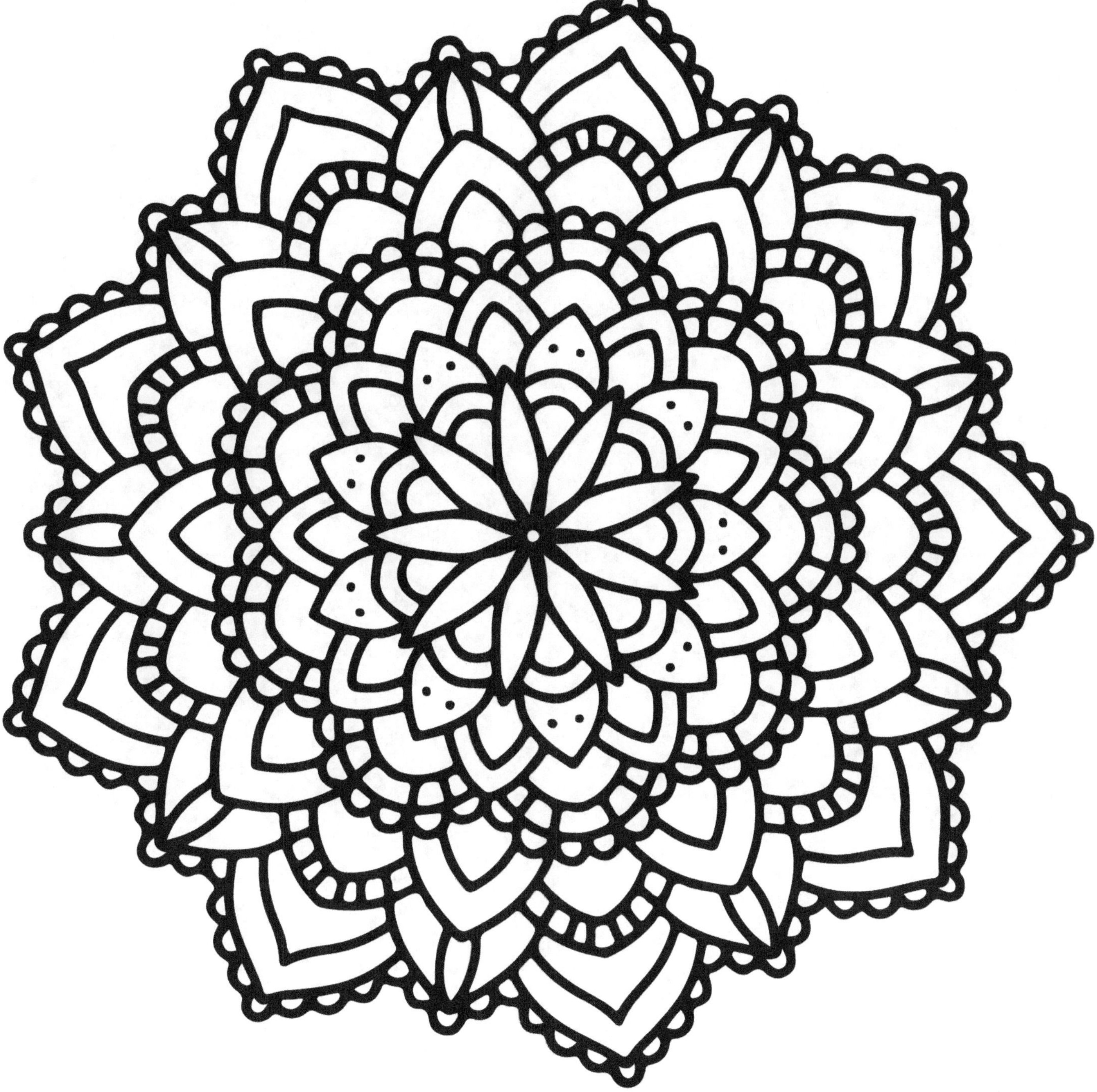

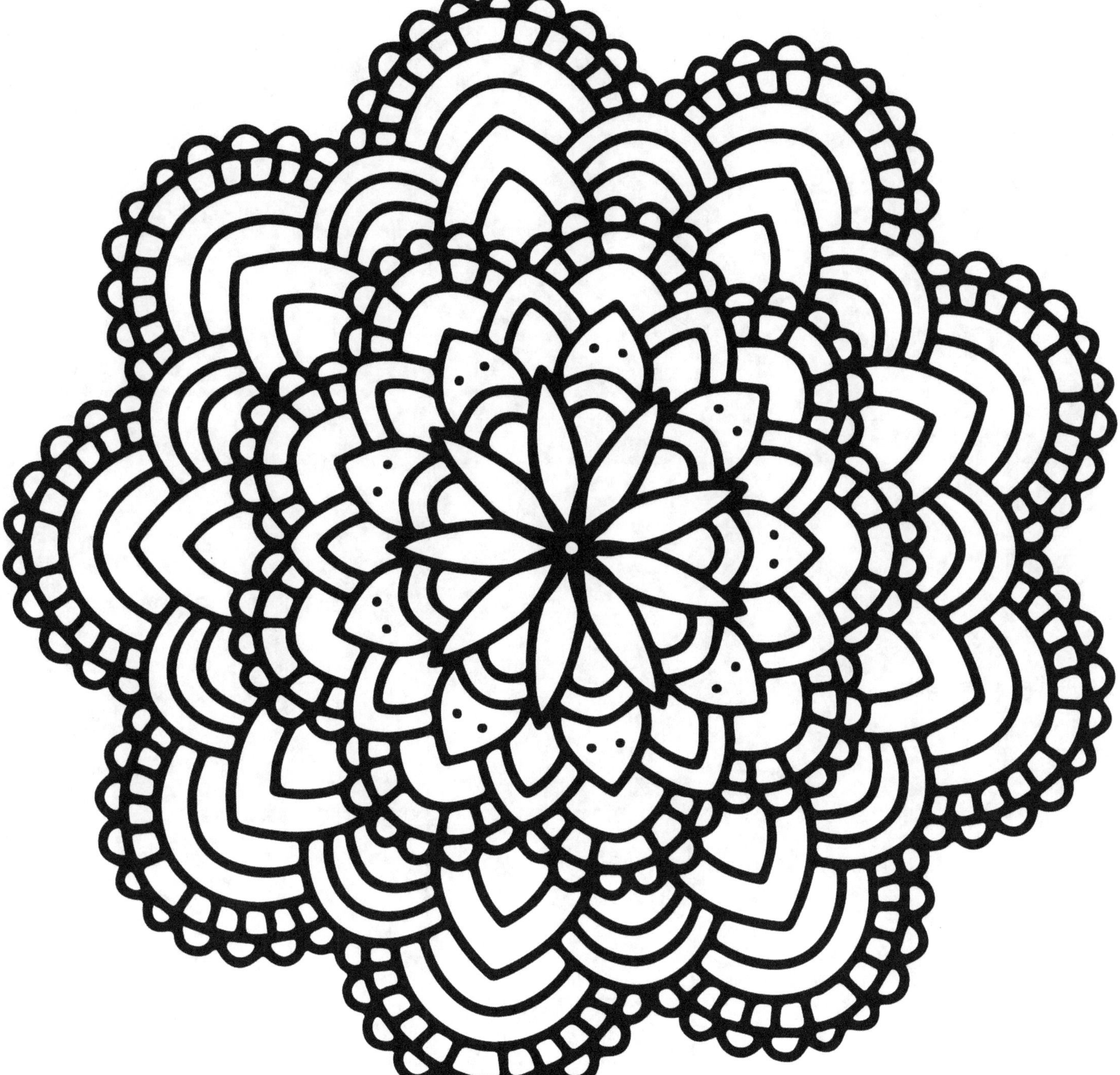

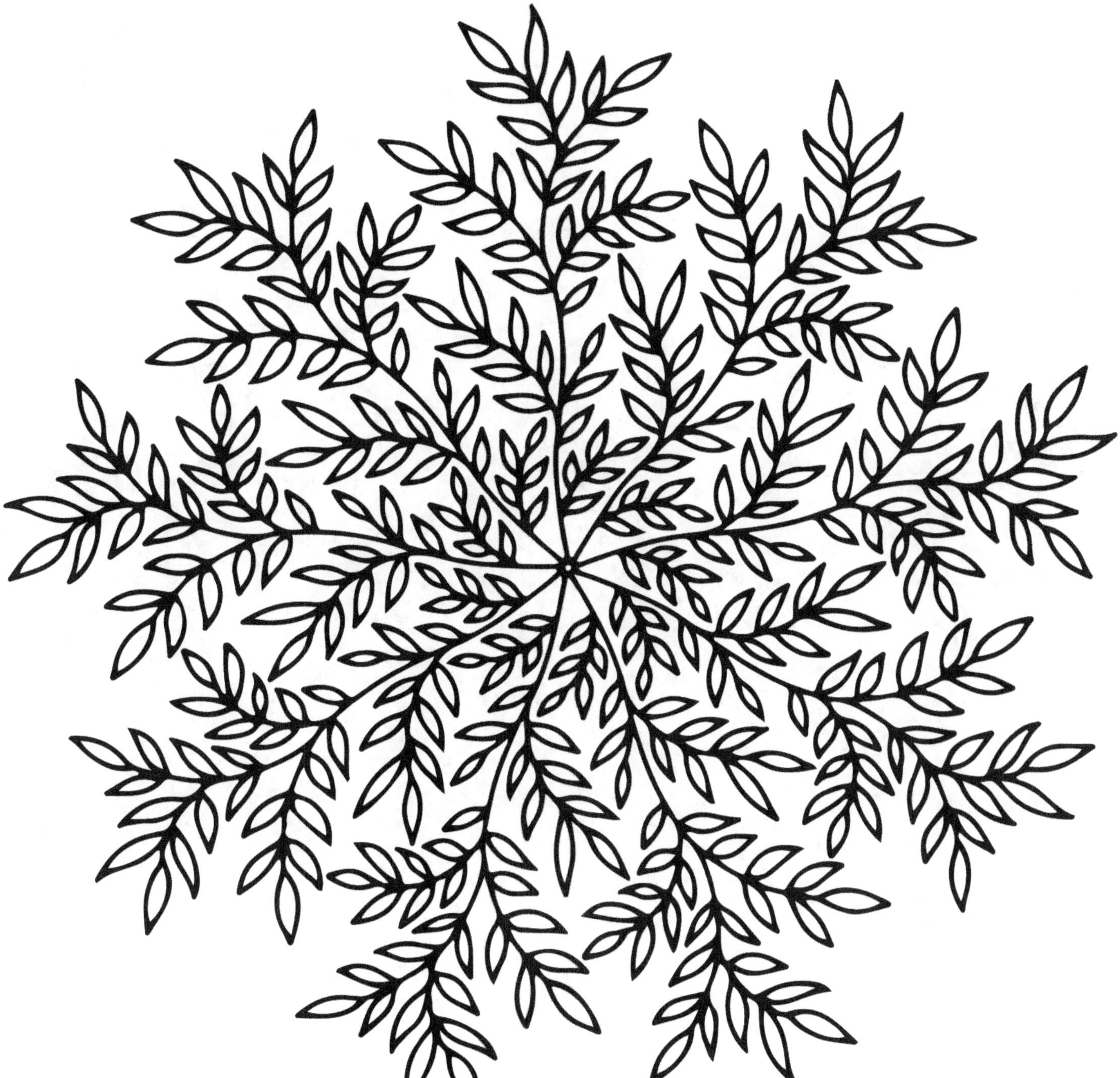

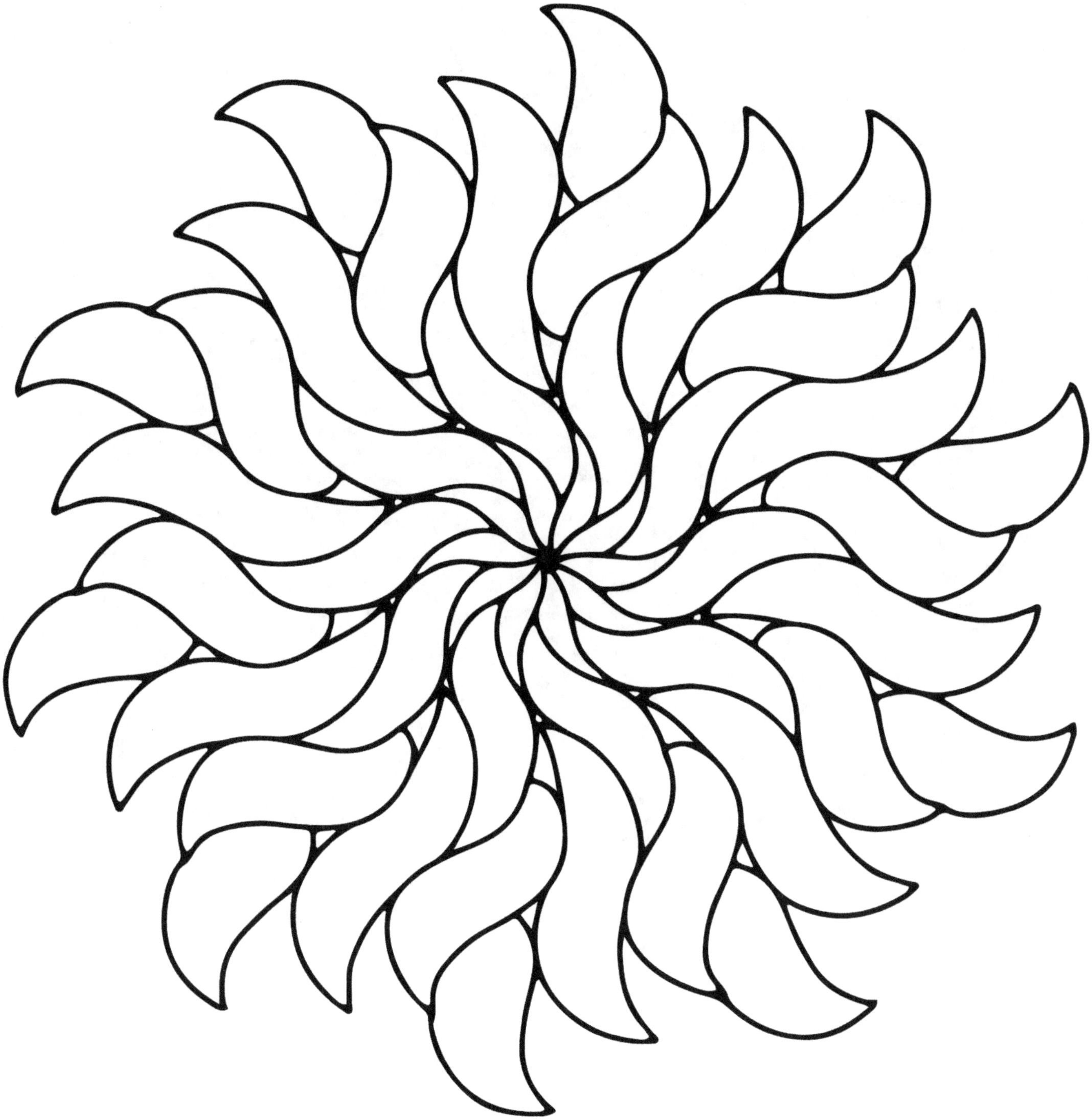

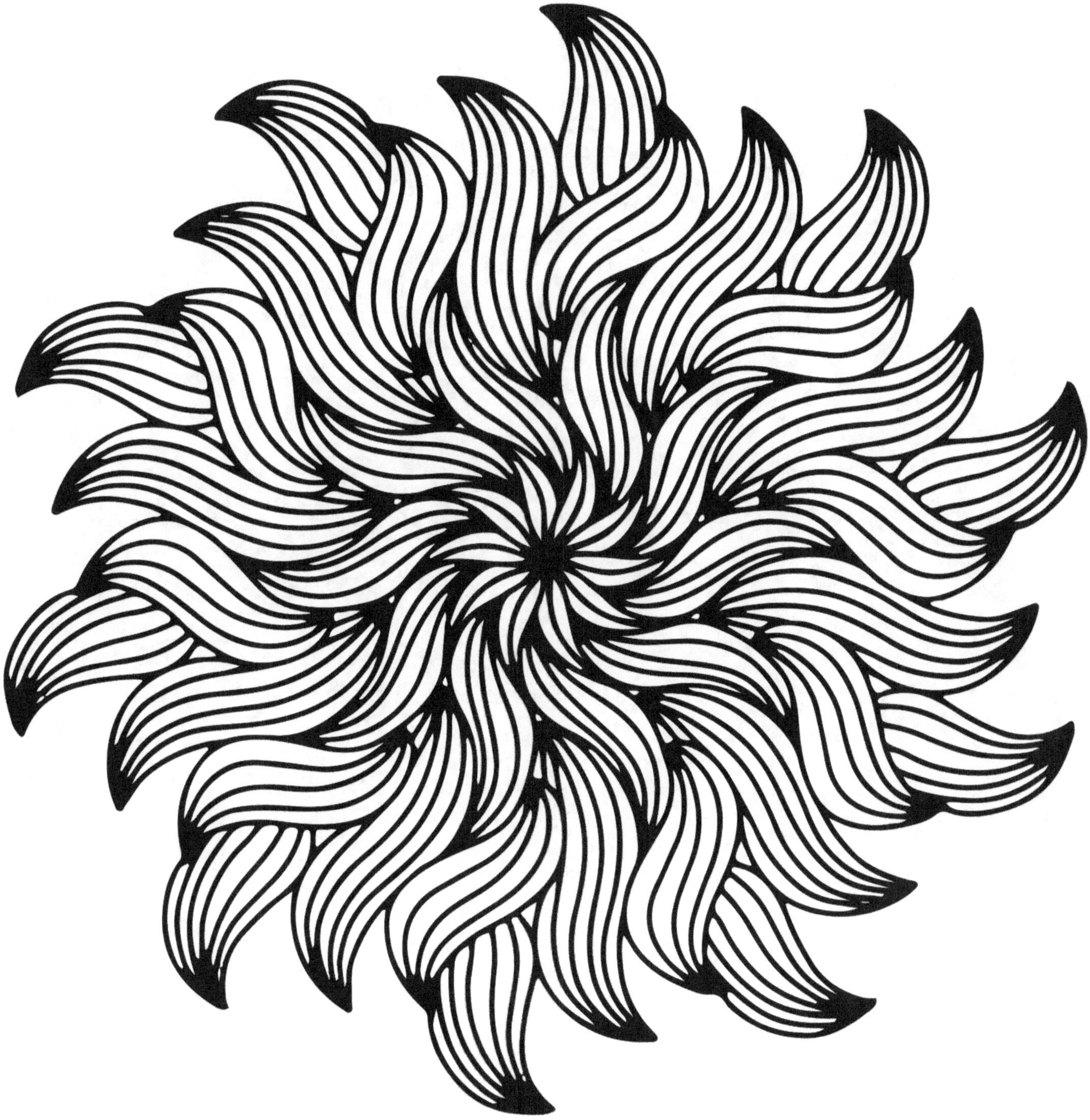

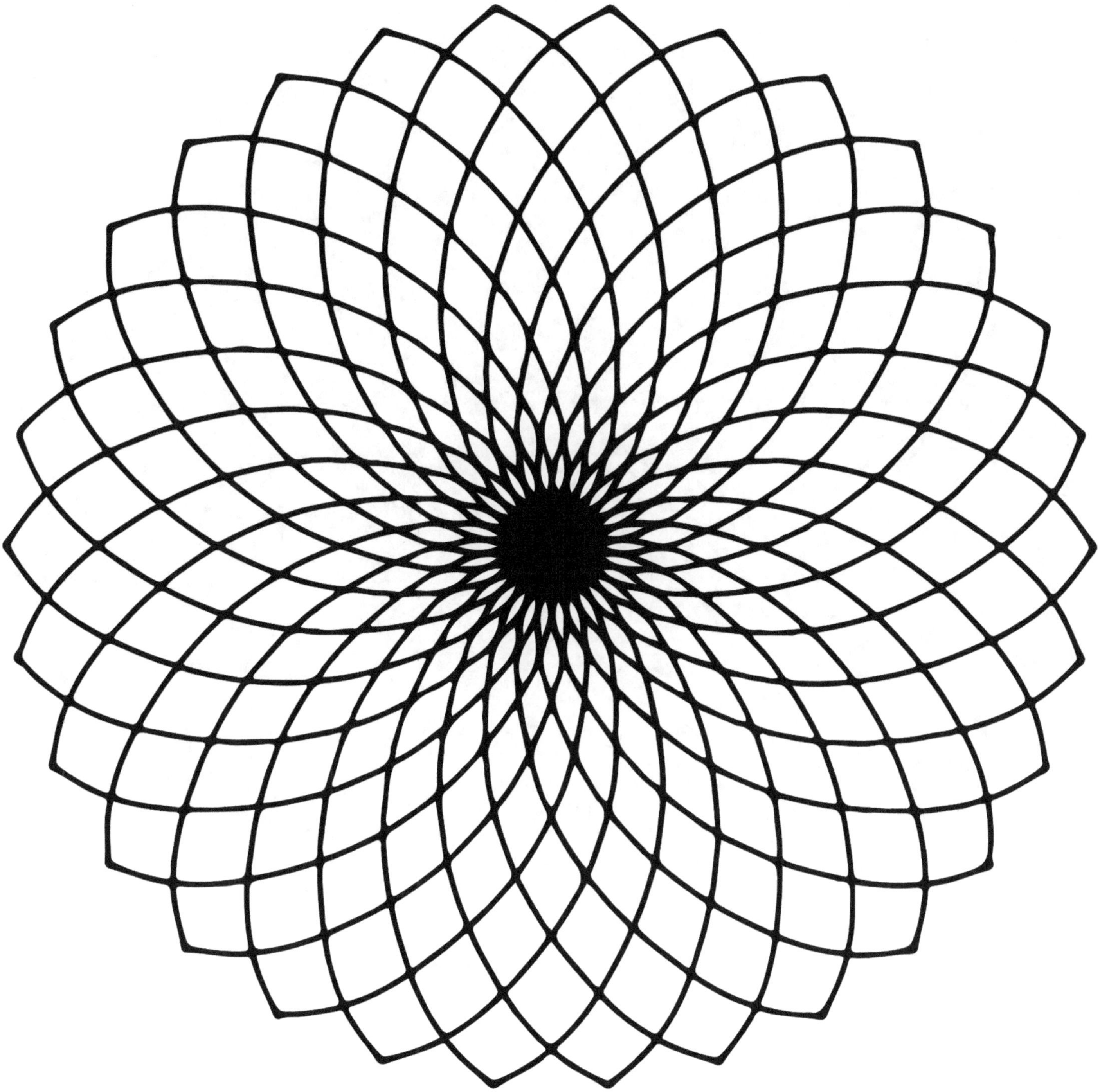

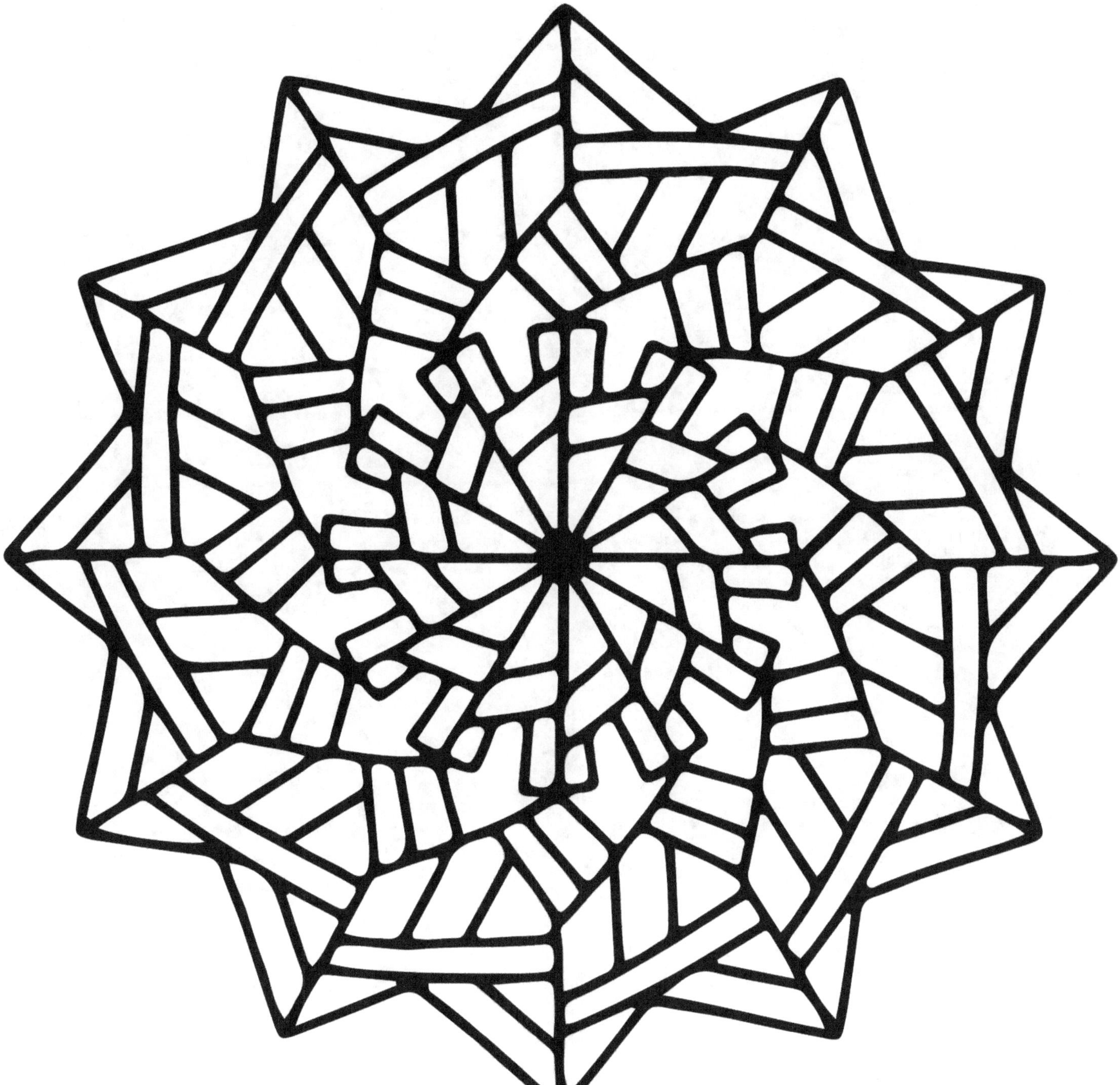

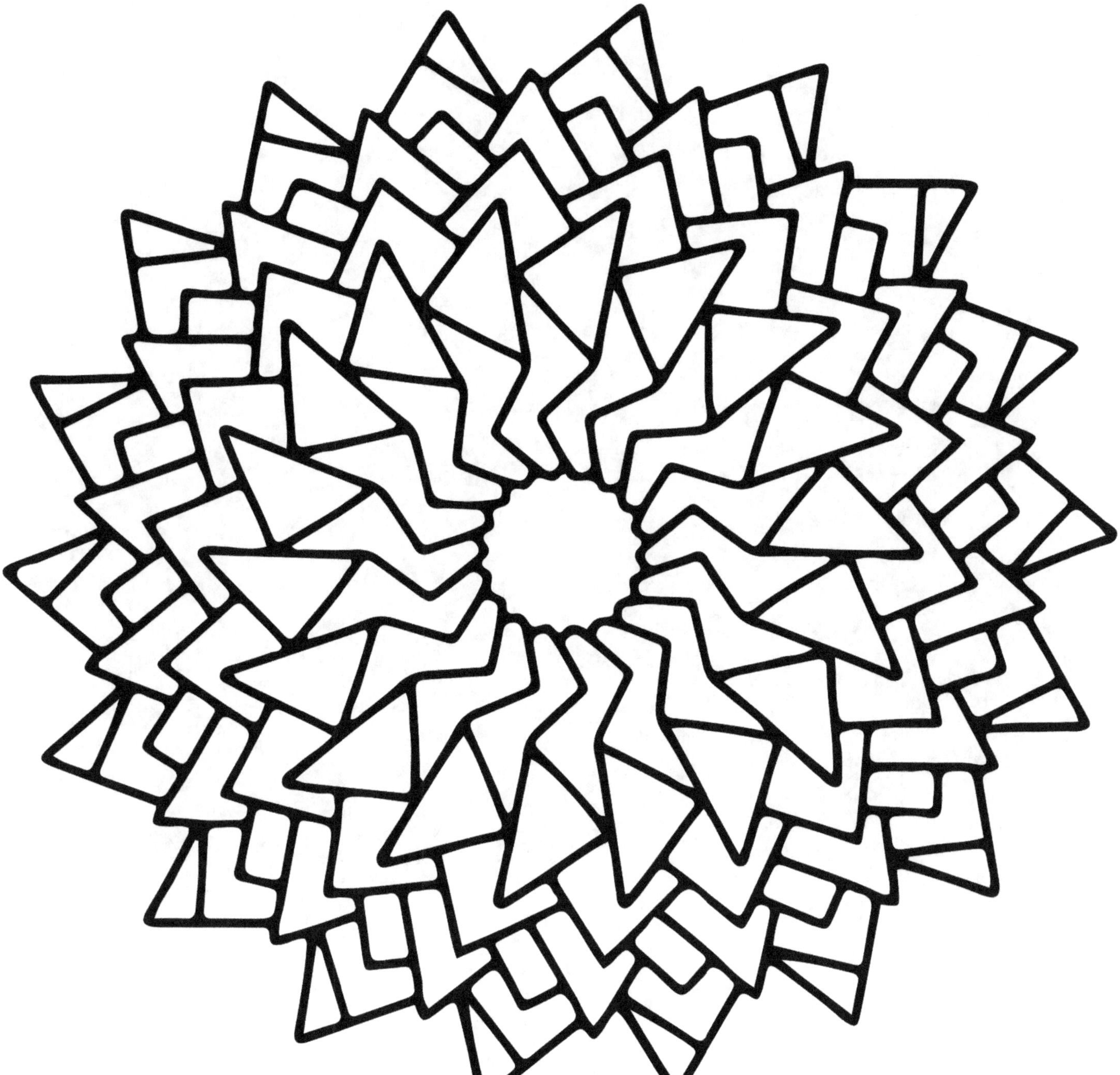

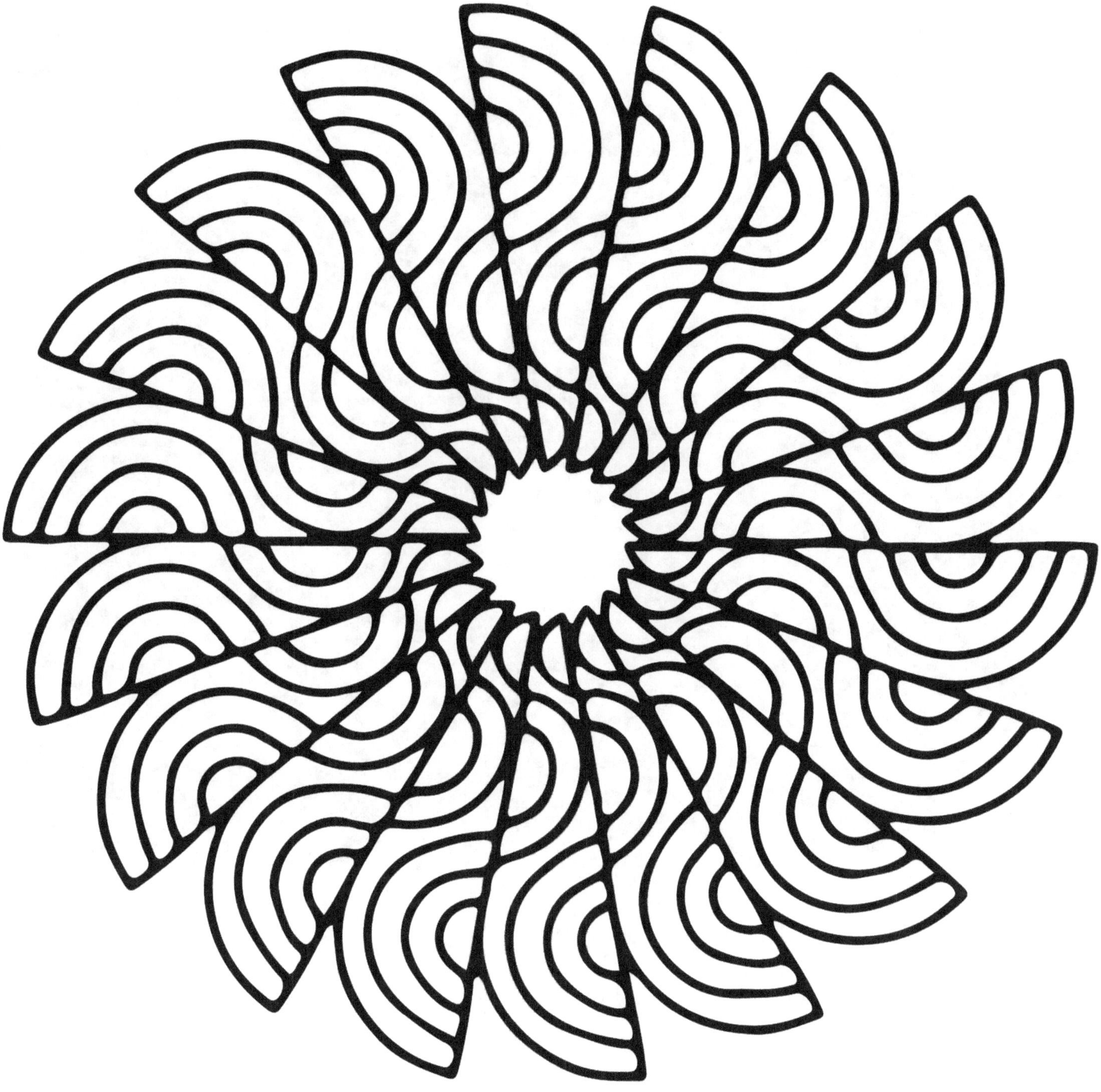

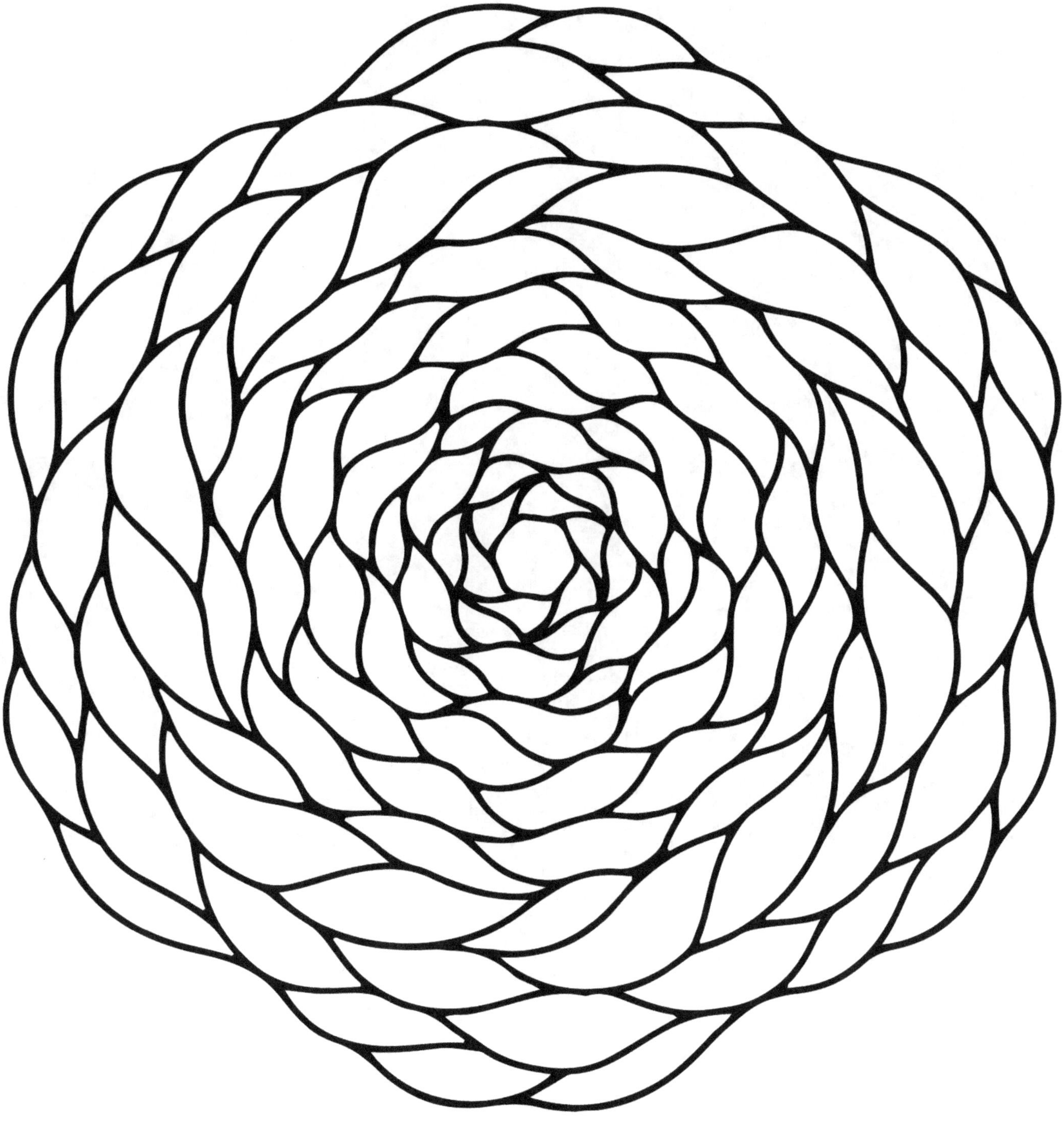

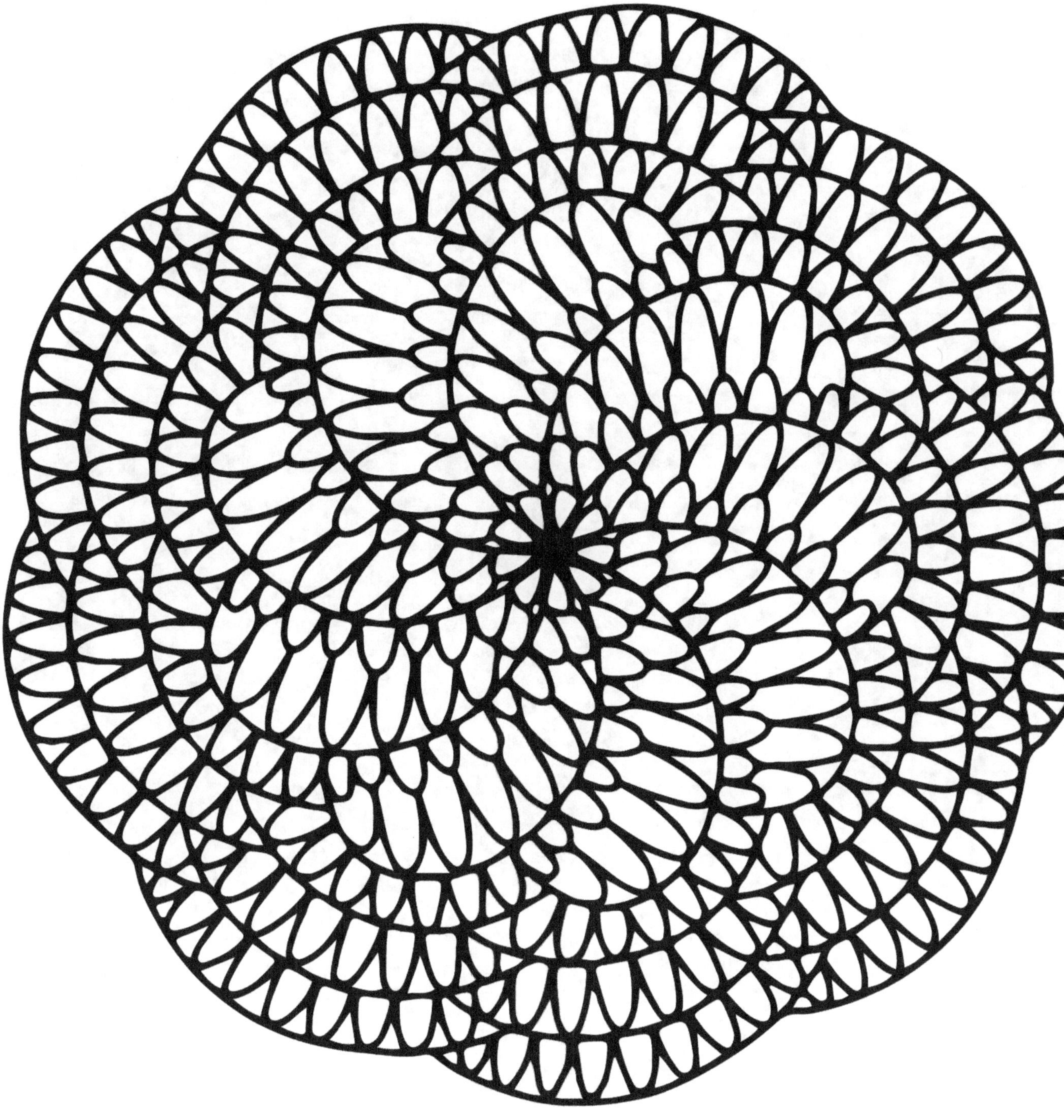

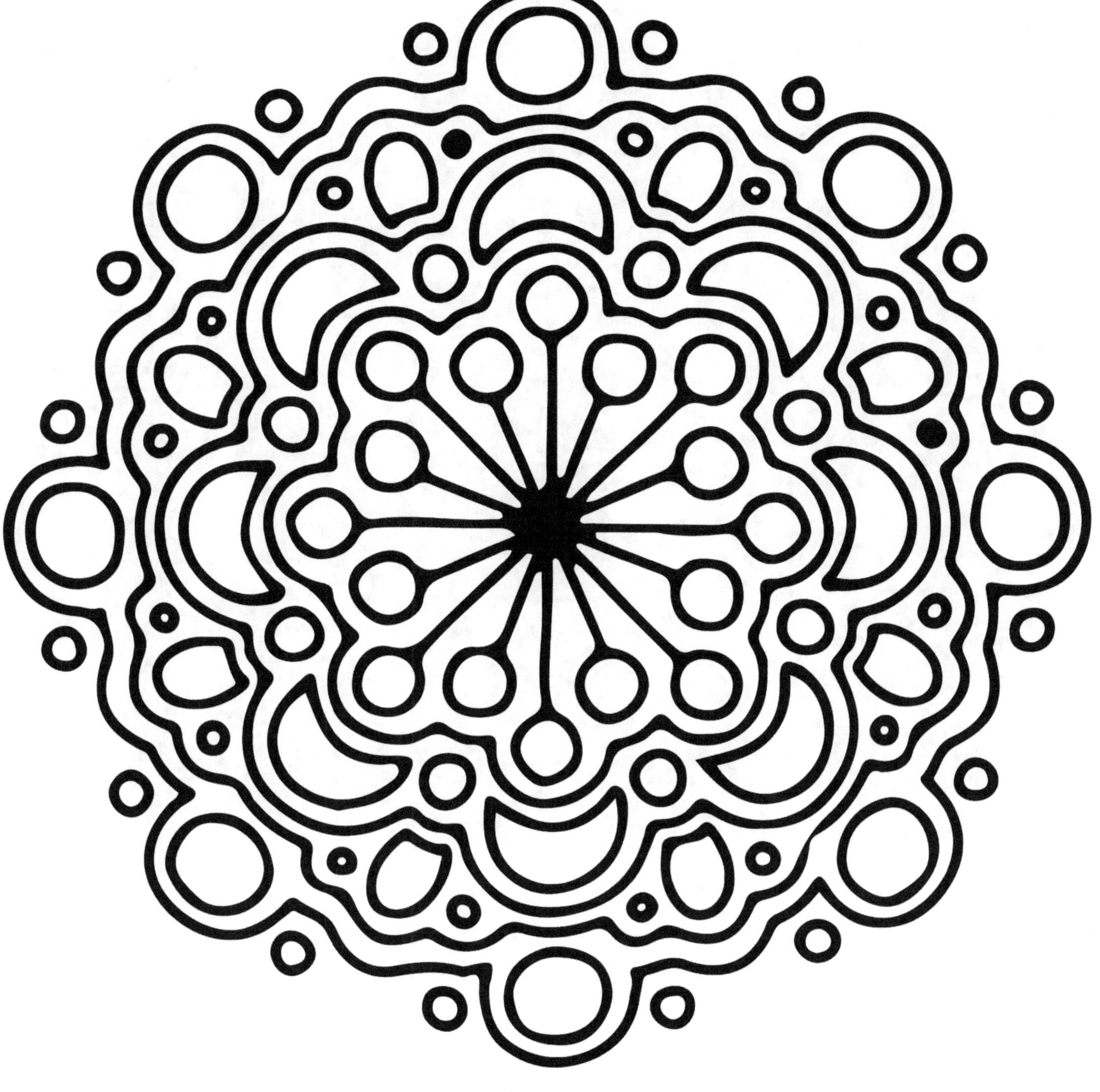

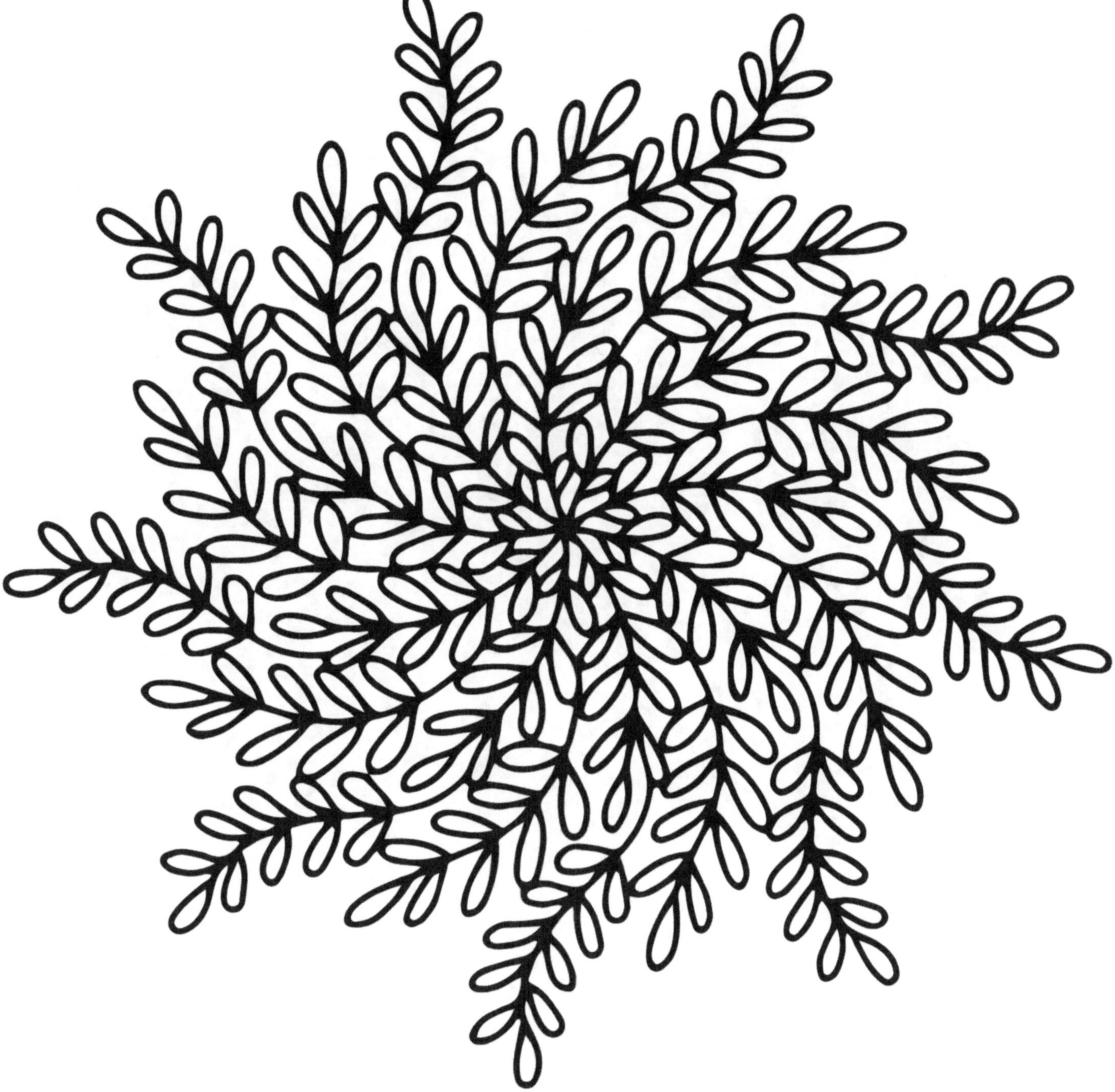

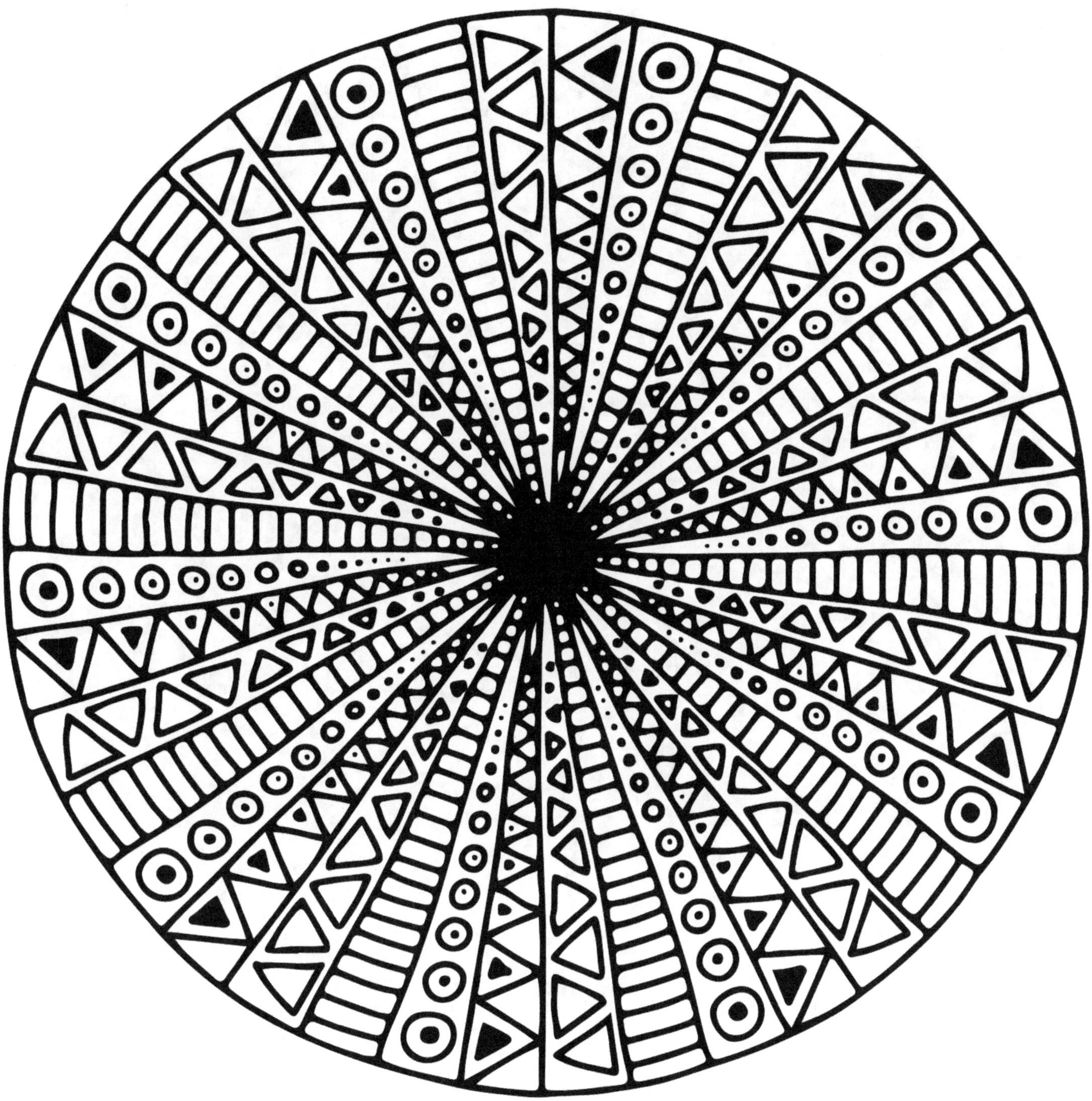

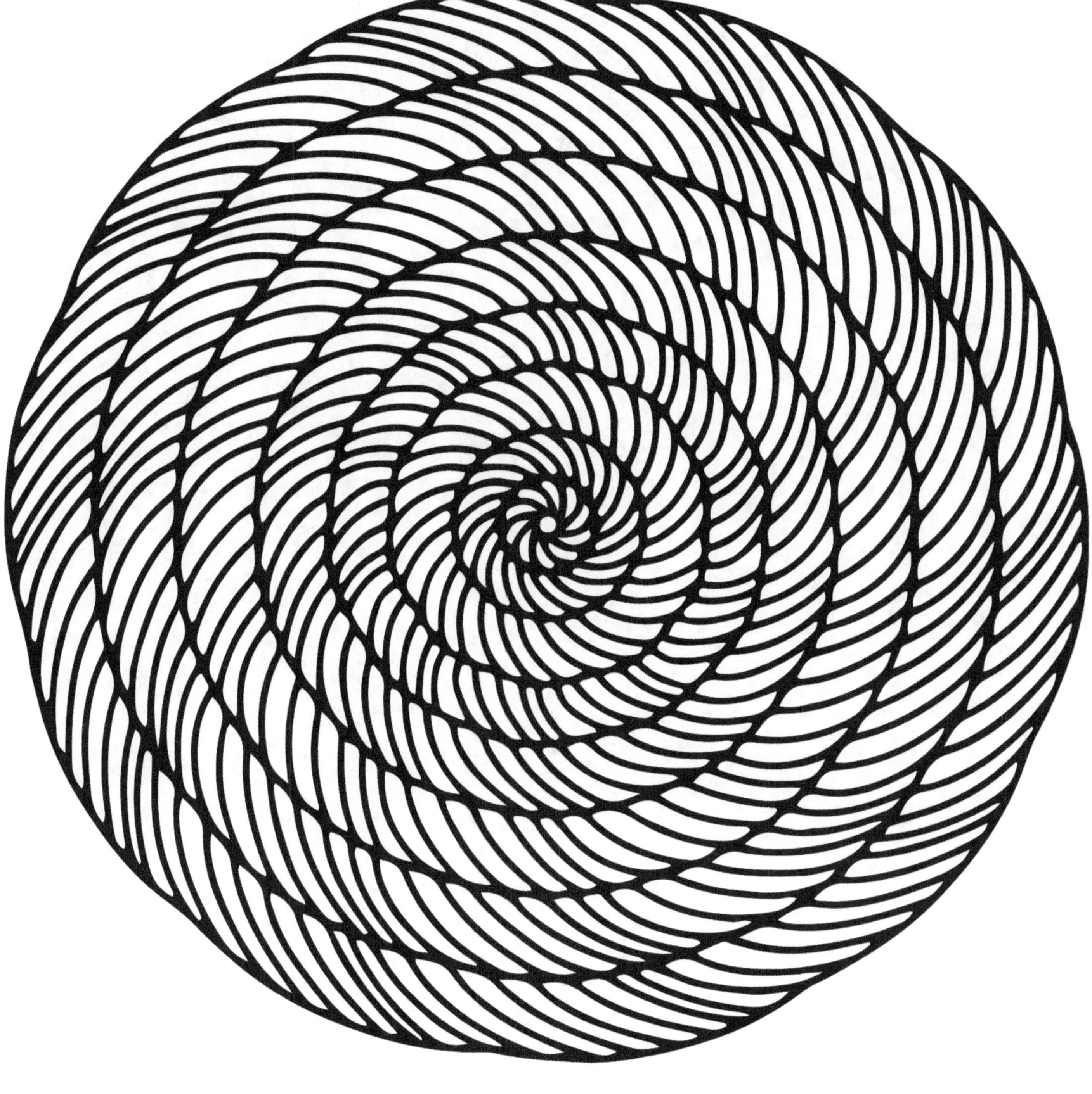

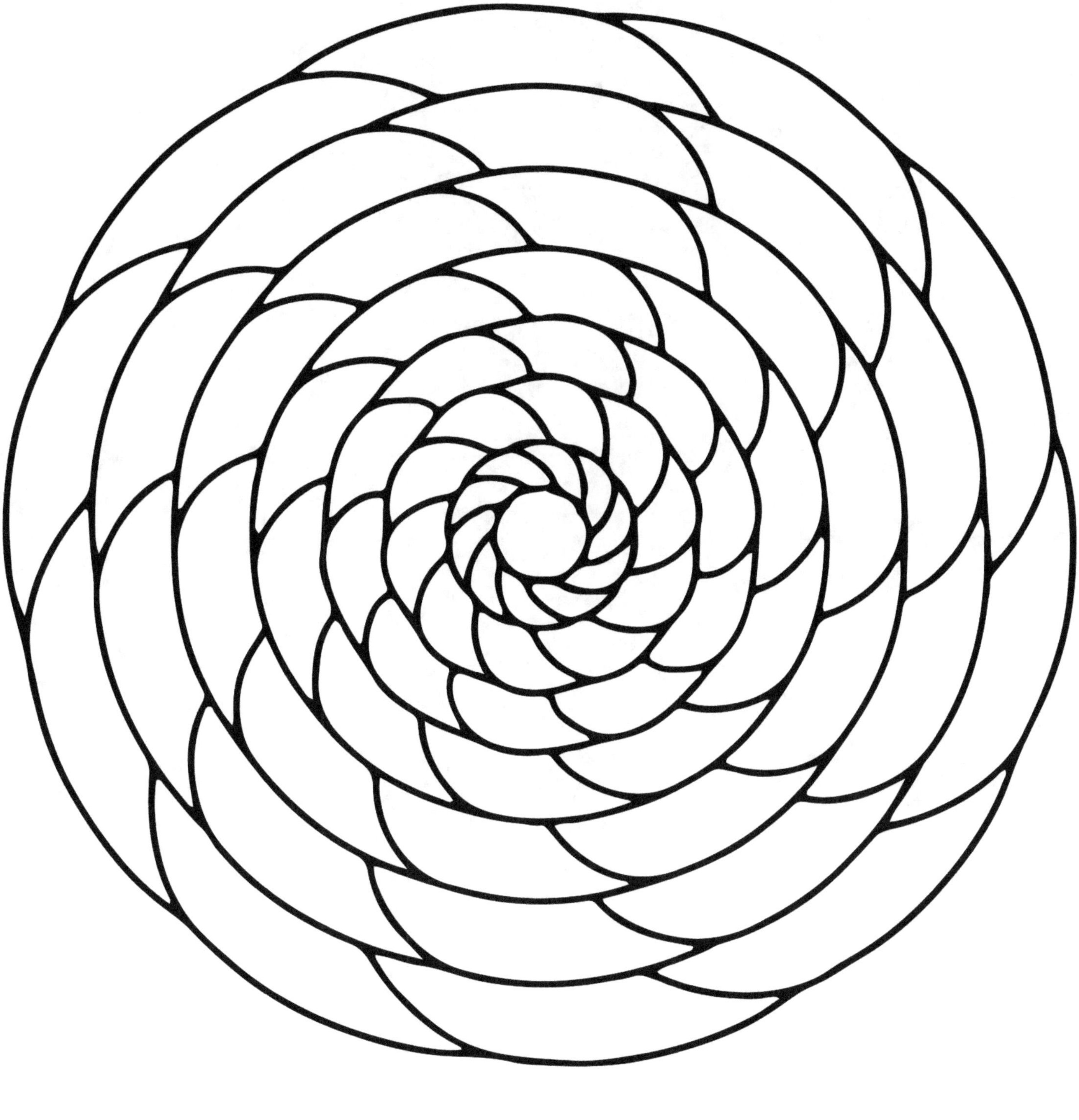

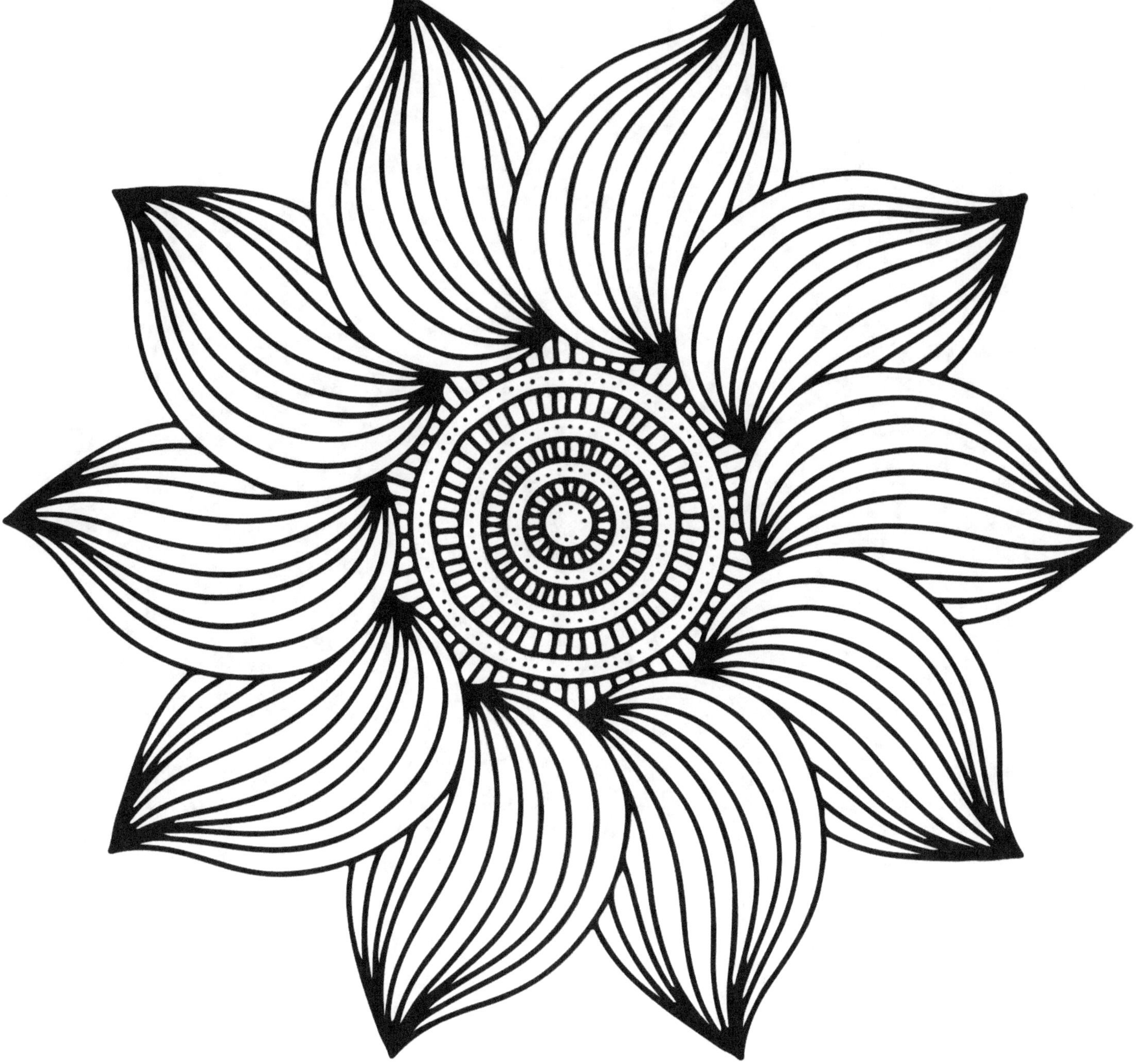

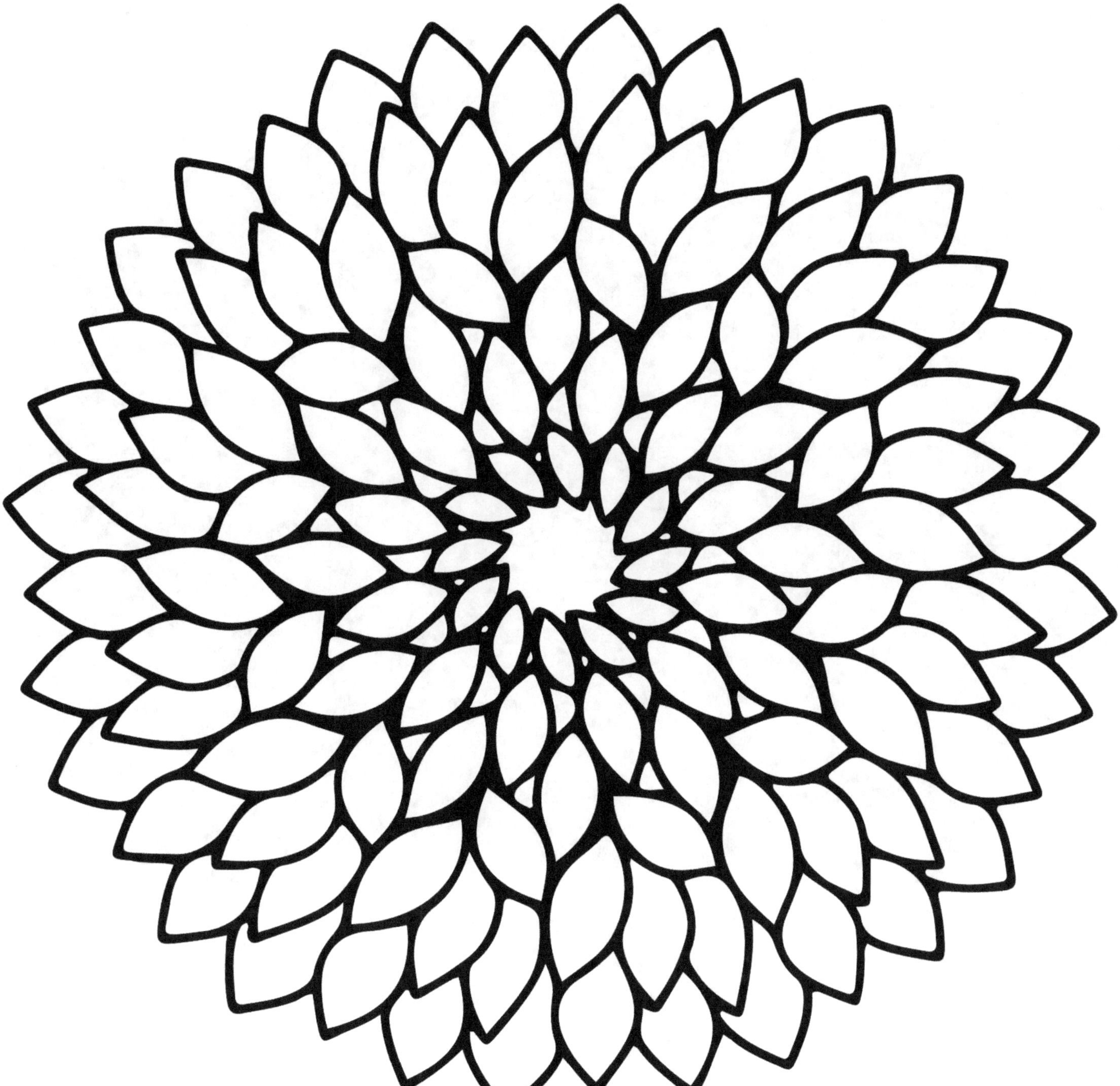

www.ingramcontent.com/pod-product-compliance
Lightning Source LLC
Chambersburg PA
CBHW081625250726
48657CB00009B/2728
* 9 7 8 1 6 9 6 5 1 9 6 7 0 *